Meaningful Quotes

Published by
Lotus Press Publishers & Distributors

Meaningful Quotes

Simar Ahuja

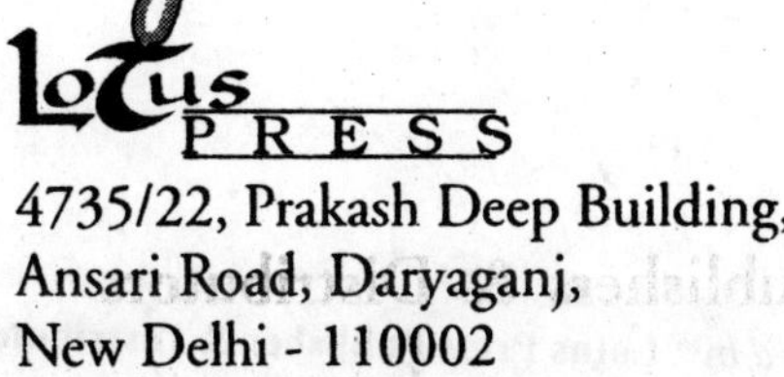

4735/22, Prakash Deep Building,
Ansari Road, Daryaganj,
New Delhi - 110002

Lotus Press : Publishers & Distributors
Unit No. 220, 2nd Floor, 4735/22, Prakash Deep Building,
Ansari Road, Darya Ganj, New Delhi- 110002
Ph.: 23280047, 98118-38000
• E-mail : lotuspress1984@gmail.com
www.lotuspress.co.in

Meaningful Quotes

ISBN: 978-81-8382-233-6

Printed & Published by : **Lotus Press Publisher & Distributors,** New Delhi-02

Preface

In several times of your day-to-day life, as a human being, you wear several hats at once, there is much chaos and disorder surrounding your life. Then you are wanting to regain some peace, clarity and inspiration. Sometimes, it is simply not possible to hear of meaningful and inspiring quotes from the people living in your environment. Instead, negativity prevails in the air. People complain and moan constantly about their lives and you desperately need to hear of some positive and inspirational messages.

In this book you can find some meaningful thoughts and words to soothe your soul. There is wit, realities, encouragement and certainly plenty of enthusiasm packed into these meaningful quotations. Be inspired by the wisdom of great personalities and may you gain the needed motivation to pursue whatever you dream of achieving in your life. Time passes real quickly and you may find the courage within you to go after your heart's desires. And when the time comes for you to look back at your life, may you be deeply grateful that you've led a life that has purpose and meaning to you.

It is hoped that the wisdom of these meaningful quotes will raise your spirits and make you revel in the wonders of living a meaningful life.

-Author

Contents

1

Ability Quotes

Effective communicators often blend-in famous quotations into their discourses. The following are some ability quotations that can motivate your listeners. Laced with profound insights, these ability quotations and their authors add credibility to your speech.

The king is the man who can.

– Thomas Carlyle

Knowing what you cannot do is more important than knowing what you can do. In fact, that's good taste.

– Lucille Ball

The extent of your consciousness is limited only by your ability to love and to embrace with your love the space around you, and all it contains

– Ken Carey

The first requisite for success is the ability to apply your physical and mental energies to one problem incessantly without growing weary.

– Thomas A. Edison

Big jobs usually go to the men who prove their ability to outgrow small ones.

– Ralph Waldo Emerson

The ability to delude yourself may be an important survival tool.

– Jane Wagner

What women have to stand on squarely is not their ability to see the world in the way men see it, but the importance and validity of their seeing it in some other way.

— ***Mary Austin***

The ability to reduce everything to simple fundamental laws does not imply the ability to start from those laws and reconstruct the universe.

— ***Philip W. Anderson***

Success is the ability to rise above principle.

— ***Gerald Barzan***

The lust of human freedoms—the ability to chose one's attitude in a given set of circumstances.

— ***Viktor E. Frankl***

Tact is the ability to describe others as they see themselves.

— ***Abraham Lincoln***

Liberty, taking the word in its concrete sense, consists in the ability to choose.

— ***Simone Weil***

The ability to quote is a serviceable substitute for wit.

— ***W. Somerset Maugham***

Nothing has such power to broaden the mind as the ability to investigate systematically and truly all that comes under your observation in life.

— ***Marcus Aurelius***

Self-respect is the fruit of discipline; the sense of dignity grows with the ability to say no to oneself

— ***Abraham J. Heschel***

2

About Me Quotes

Life is an eternal quest about knowing oneself. It is time to challenge yourself, to rediscover your hidden traits, talents, and tendencies. Several inconvenient questions, which you have swept under the carpet, might resurface. Here is a collection of "about me" quotes. Each noted author has revealed her or his unique qualities. When you read these "about me" quotes, you will find the inspiration to ask yourself "Is that true about me?"

> I am the only person in the world I should like to know thoroughly.
>
> — *Oscar Wilde*

> I do my thing and you do yours. I am not in this world to live up to your expectations, and you are not in this world to live up to mine. You are you and I am I, and if by chance we find each other, then it is beautiful. If not, it can't be helped.
>
> — *Frederick Perls*

> I am enough of an artist to draw freely upon my imagination.
>
> — *Albert Einstein*

> I like to be a free spirit. Some don't like that, but that's the way I am.
>
> — *Princess Diana*

I am only a public entertainer who understands his time.

— Pablo Picasso

The deep root of failure in our lives is to think, 'Oh how useless and powerless I am.' It is essential to think strongly and forcefully, 'I can do it,' without boasting or fretting.

— Tenzin Gyatso, the 14th Dalai Lama

I am not myself in any degree ashamed of having changed my opinions.

— Bertrand Russell

I am my own heroine.

— Marie Bashkirtseff

I am one of the people who love the why of things.

— Catherine the Great

When I let go of what I am, I become what I might be.

— Lao Tzu

I am certainly not one of those who need to be prodded. In fact, if anything, I am the prod.

— Winston Churchill

I am not only a pacifist but a militant pacifist. I am willing to fight for peace. Nothing will end war unless the people themselves refuse to go to war."

— Albert Einstein

I am so clever that sometimes I don't understand a single word of what I am saying.

— Oscar Wilde

I am extraordinarily patient, provided I get my own way in the end.

— Margaret Thatcher

A friend is one who takes me for what I am.

— Henry David Thoreau

To say "I love you" one must first be able to say the "I."

— ***Ayn Rand***

I am the state.

— ***Louis XIV***

I am the greatest, I said that even before I knew I was.

— ***Muhammad Ali***

Without knowing what I am and why I am here, life is impossible.

— ***Leo Tolstoy***

I am the miracle.

— ***Buddha***

I am neither especially clever nor especially gifted. I am only very, very curious

— ***Albert Einstein***

3

Abdul Kalam Quotes

Dr. A. P. J. Abdul Kalam, was the eleventh President of India, serving from 2002 to 2006. Totally dedicated to the nation, he holds a first world dream for the third world nation. His vision is to make India a developed country. He has given his plan of action and a road map for realising his vision. He has articulated his thoughts in his three books: *India 2020: A Vision for the New Millennium, Wings of Fire: An Autobiography of A. P. J. Abdul Kalam* and *Ignited Minds: Unleashing the Power Within India*. India has already started looking to Dr. Kalam for inspiration and guidance. Some of the meaningful quotes by Dr. Abdul Kalam are given below.

Be more dedicated to making solid achievements than in running after swift but synthetic happiness.

Climbing to the top demands strength, whether it is to the top of Mount Everest or to the top of your career.

Educationists should build the capacities of the spirit of inquiry, creativity, entrepreneurial and moral leadership among students and become their role model.

Great dreams of great dreamers are always transcended.

I was willing to accept what I couldn't change.

If we are not free, no one will respect us.

Let us sacrifice our today so that our children can have a better tomorrow.

Life is a difficult game. You can win it only by retaining your birthright to be a person.

Look at the sky. We are not alone. The whole universe is friendly to us and conspires only to give the best to those who dream and work.

Man needs his difficulties because they are necessary to enjoy success.

No religion has mandated killing others as a requirement for its sustenance or promotion.

Those who cannot work with their hearts achieve but a hollow, half-hearted success that breeds bitterness all around.

To succeed in your mission, you must have single-minded devotion to your goal.

In this world, fear has no place. Only strength respects strength.

We have not invaded anyone. We have not conquered anyone. We have not grabbed their land, their culture, their history and tried to enforce our way of life on them.

We must think and act like a nation of a billion people and not like that of a million people. Dream, dream, dream!

We should not give up and we should not allow the problem to defeat us.

We will be remembered only if we give to our younger generation a prosperous and safe India, resulting out of economic prosperity coupled with civilisational heritage.

You have to dream before your dreams can come true.

4

Abraham Lincoln Quotes

Abraham Lincoln is seen as one of the foremost symbols of American democracy. Born to a nondescript family, his life proved that in America any boy can grow up to be President one day. This is a collection of Abraham Lincoln quotes that reflect his beliefs and values.

The Almighty has his own purposes.

It is not best to swap horses while crossing the river.

Truth is generally the best vindication against slander.

Beware of rashness, but with energy and sleepless vigilance go forward and give us victories.

Men are not flattered by being shown that there has been a difference of purpose between the Almighty and them.

A house divided against itself cannot stand.

In giving freedom to the slave we assure freedom to the free—honorable alike in what we give and what we preserve.

Let us have faith that right makes might; and in that faith let us to the end, dare to do our duty as we understand it.

A friend is one who has the same enemies as you have.

Nobody has ever expected me to be President. In my poor, lean lank face nobody has ever seen that any cabbages were sprouting.

You can fool some of the people all of the time, and all of the people some of the time, but you can not fool all of the people all of the time.

A woman is the only thing I am afraid of that I know will not hurt me.

All my life I have tried to pluck a thistle and plant a flower wherever the flower would grow in thought and mind.

Always bear in mind that your own resolution to succeed is more important than any other.

Avoid popularity if you would have peace.

Common looking people are the best in the world: that is the reason the Lord makes so many of them.

5

Achievement Quotes

Watch an athlete who runs a quick mile. His achievement inspires him to beat his own record. As he improves, he sets loftier targets for himself. Such is the "vicious" circle of achievement. But what happens if he were to fail? Does he give up and go back? Failure causes disappointment, but with the right attitude, we can turn failures into stepping stones to success. Find inspiration in the achievement quotes given below. These achievement sayings teach you how to find a silver lining in every grey cloud.

> Every man who accomplishes things sees first in his mind what he wishes to do. He puts away all doubt. It makes no difference how small or how large the thing you want to do may be; if you have an unlimited confidence in your ability to do it, you will do
>
> — *Charles Fillmore*

> In time of difficulties, we must not lose sight of our achievements.
>
> — *Mao Tse-tung*

> The roots of true achievement lie in the will to become the best that you can become.
>
> — *Harold Taylor*

> Achievement is largely the product of steadily raising one's levels of aspiration and expectation.
>
> — *Jack Nicklaus*

Failures are finger posts on the road to achievement.

— ***C. S. Lewis***

The awareness of the ambiguity of one's highest achievements (as well as one's deepest failures) is a definite symptom of maturity.

— ***Paul Tillich***

Simplicity is the final achievement. After one has played a vast quantity of notes and more notes, it is simplicity that emerges as the crowning reward of art.

— ***Frederic Chopin***

Dissatisfaction with possession and achievement is one of the requisites to further achievement.

— ***John Hope***

Press on—nothing can take the place of persistence. Talent will not; nothing is more common than unsuccessful men with talent. Genius will not; unrewarded genius is almost a proverb. Education will not; the world is full of educated derelicts. Perseverance and determination alone are omnipotent.

— ***Calvin Coolidge***

Achievement seems to be connected with action. Successful men and women keep moving. They make mistakes, but they don't quit.

— ***Conrad Hilton***

There are no shortcuts to life's greatest achievements.

— ***Anonymous***

Periods of tranquility are seldom prolific of creative achievement. Mankind has to be stirred up.

— ***Alfred North Whitehead***

Man is not the sum of what he has but the totality of what he does not yet have, of what he might have.

— ***Jean-Paul Sartre***

6

Action Quotes

Often it is about getting out of the endless loop of thinking and getting into action. These quotes should motivate you to do that.

> It is common sense to take a method and try it. If it fails, admit it frankly and try another. But above all, try something.
>
> ***Franklin D. Roosevelt***

> It is surprising what a man can do when he has to, and how little most men will do when they don't have to.
>
> ***Walter Linn***

> It is the nature of thought to find its way into action.
>
> ***Christian Nevell Bovee***

> It is time for us all to stand and cheer for the doer, the achiever—the one who recognises the challenge and does something about it.
>
> ***Vincent Lombardi***

> It takes less time to do things right than to explain why you did it wrong.
>
> ***Henry Wadsworth Longfellow***

> I've found that luck is quite predictable. If you want more luck, take more chances. Be more active. Show up more often.
>
> ***Brian Tracy***

Just as a flower, which seems beautiful has color but no perfume, so are the fruitless words of a man who speaks them but does them not.

Dhammapada

Just Do It.

Nike

Just do what you do best.

Red Auerbach

Knowing is not enough; we must apply. Willing is not enough; we must do

Johann von Goethe

The best way to finish an unpleasant task is to get started.

Anonymous

Don't wait. The time will never be just right.

Napoleon Hill

I have been impressed with the urgency of doing. Knowing is not enough; we must apply. Being willing is not enough; we must do.

Leonardo da Vinci

Everything you want is out there waiting for you to ask. Everything you want also wants you. But you have to take action to get it.

Jules Renard

Success seems to be connected with action. Successful people keep moving. They make mistakes, but they don't quit.

Conrad Hilton

You may never know what results come of your action, but if you do nothing there will be no result.

Mahatma Gandhi

7

Adversity Quotes

Adversities are part of life and they usually bring with them big lessons for us to learn, grow and shape up as an individual, as a woman in our own right. The adversity quotes given below remind us that in everyone's life, there's difficulties, trials and problems. These quotes encourage you on the journey of life.

A problem is a chance for you to do your best.

— ***Duke Ellington***

Adversity is like a strong wind. It tears away from us all but the things that cannot be torn, so that we see ourselves as we really are.

— ***Arthur Golden, Memoirs of a Geisha***

Birds sing after a storm; why shouldn't people feel as free to delight in whatever remains to them?

— ***Rose F. Kennedy***

Count the garden by the flowers, never by the leaves that fall. Count your life with smiles and not the tears that roll.

— ***Author Unknown***

Each difficult moment has the potential to open my eyes and open my heart.

— ***Myla Kabat-Zinn***

Every adversity, every failure, every heartache carries with it the seed of an equal or greater benefit.

— ***Napoleon Hill***

Every defeat, every heartbreak, every loss, contains its own seed, its own lesson on how to improve your performance the next time.

— ***Og Mandino***

Every trial endured and weathered in the right spirit makes a soul nobler and stronger than it was before.

— ***James Buckham***

Have the courage to face a difficulty lest it kick you harder than you bargained for.

— ***Stanislaus I, Maxims***

I ask not for a lighter burden, but for broader shoulders.

— ***Jewish Proverb***

I don't like people who have never fallen or stumbled. Their virtue is lifeless and it isn't of much value. Life hasn't revealed its beauty to them.

— ***Boris Pasternak***

I have had dreams and I have had nightmares, but I have conquered my nightmares because of my dreams.

— ***Jonas Salk***

I have sometimes been wildly, despairingly, acutely miserable, but through it all I still know quite certainly that just to be alive is a grand thing.

— ***Agatha Christie***

I owe much to my friends; but, all things considered, it strikes me that I owe even more to my enemies. The real person springs life under a sting even better than under a caress.

— ***André Gide***

If we will be quiet and ready enough, we shall find compensation in every disappointment.

— ***Henry David Thoreau***

If you can find a path with no obstacles, it probably doesn't lead anywhere.

— Frank A. Clark

If you don't like something change it; if you can't change it, change the way you think about it.

— Mary Engelbreit

Life is thickly sown with thorns, and I know no other remedy than to pass quickly through them. The longer we dwell on our misfortunes, the greater is their power to harm us.

— Voltaire

Patience and perseverance have a magical effect before which difficulties disappear and obstacles vanish.

— John Quincy Adams

Perhaps all the dragons of our lives are princesses who are only waiting to see us once beautiful and brave.

— Rainer Maria Rilke

The gem cannot be polished without friction nor man without trials.

— Confucius

The greater the difficulty, the more glory in surmounting it. Skillful pilots gain their reputation from storms and tempests.

— Epictetus

We shall draw from the heart of suffering itself the means of inspiration and survival.

— Winston Churchill

You may not realise it when it happens, but a kick in the teeth may be the best thing in the world for you.

— Walt Disney

Your most unhappy customers are your greatest source of learning.

— Bill Gates

8

Aging Quotes

Getting old is a natural process where things are slowing down, and you'll begin to see that the sparkle in your heart and the twinkle in your eyes make you beautiful in a way that's not achievable in youth. Go through the growing old quotes given below. Many of them are light-hearted, some are funny and a few are inspiring.

About the only thing that comes to us without effort is old age.

— *Gloria Pitzer*

Age does not diminish the extreme disappointment of having a scoop of ice cream fall from the cone.

— *Jim Fiebig*

Age is an issue of mind over matter. If you don't mind, it doesn't matter.

— *Mark Twain*

'Age' is the acceptance of a term of years. But maturity is the glory of years.

— *Martha Graham*

The best way to keep kids at home is to make the home a pleasant atmosphere...and let the air out of their tires.

— *Dorothy Parker*

The first sign of maturity is the discovery that the volume knob also turns to the left.

— *Jerry M. Wright*

The great thing about getting older is that you don't lose all the other ages you've been.

— ***Madeleine L'Engle***

The more you complain, the longer God lets you live.

— ***Author Unknown***

The time to begin most things is ten years ago.

— ***Mignon McLaughlin***

The older you get, the more you tell it like it used to be.

— ***Author Unknown***

The great secret that all old people share is that you really haven't changed in 70 or 80 years. Your body changes, but you don't change at all.

— ***Doris Lessing***

Time wounds all heels.

— ***Dorothy Parker***

To keep the heart unwrinkled, to be hopeful, kindly, cheerful, reverent—that is to triumph over old age.

— ***Thomas Bailey Aldrich***

You don't stop laughing because you grow old. You grow old because you stop laughing.

— ***Michael Pritchard***

You can live to be a hundred if you give up all the things that make you want to live to be a hundred.

— ***Woody Allen***

You can only perceive real beauty in a person as they get older.

— ***Anouk Aimee***

You know you're getting old when you stoop to tie your shoelaces and wonder what else you could do while you're down there.

— ***George Burns***

In a dream you are never eighty.

— ***Anne Sexton***

At twenty we worry about what others think of us; at forty we don't care about what others think of us; at sixty we discover they haven't been thinking about us at all.

— ***Author Unknown***

Beautiful young people are accidents of nature, but beautiful old people are works of art.

— ***Eleanor Roosevelt***

Do not resent growing old. Many are denied the privilege.

— ***Author Unknown***

Inside every older person is a younger person wondering what happened.

— ***Jennifer Yane***

Life can only be understood backwards, but it must be lived forwards.

— ***Soren Kierkegaard***

Old age is no place for sissies.

— ***Bette Davis***

Old age isn't so bad when you consider the alternative.

— ***Maurice Chevalier***

Once you're over the hill, you begin to pick up speed.

— ***Charles M. Schulz***

The best part about being my age is in knowing how my life worked out. Sure, there's a lot more living to go, but there isn't much doubt that I'll always be the 'Dilbert guy.' Unless I go on a crime spree, in which case I'll be 'that stabbin' Dilbert guy.'

— ***Scott Adams***

9

Aim Quotes

What sets us apart from other species is that we humans are driven by ambition. Some ambitions are specific, while others are vague. A life without ambition is a waste. An aim quote that influenced me is, "Aim small, miss small." These aim quotes remind us to never stop marching towards our goal.

A goal is a dream with a deadline.

— Napoleon Hill

A person who aims at nothing is sure to hit it.

— Anonymous

A wise man will make more opportunities than he finds.

— Francis Bacon

Act like you expect to get into the end zone.

— Joe Paterno

Aim for the highest.

— Andrew Carnegie

All successful people have a goal. No one can get anywhere unless he knows where he wants to go and what he wants to be or do.

— Norman Vincent Peale

Ambition can creep as well as soar.

— Edmund Burke

All who have accomplished great things have had a great aim, have fixed their gaze on a goal which was high, one which sometimes seemed impossible.

– Orison Swett Marden

All you have to do is know where you're going. The answers will come to you of their own accord.

– Earl Nightingale

Always bear in mind that your own resolution to succeed is more important than any other one thing.

– Abraham Lincoln

Goals give you more than a reason to get up in the morning; they are an incentive to keep you going all day. Goals tend to tap the deeper resources and draw the best out of life.

– Harvey Mackay

Goals. There's not telling what you can do when you get inspired by them. There's no telling what you can do when you believe in them. There's no telling what will happen when you act upon them.

– Jim Rohn

God made man to go by motives, and he will not go without them, any more than a boat without steam or a balloon without gas.

– Henry Ward Beecher

Great ambition is the passion of a great character. Those endowed with it may perform very good or very bad acts. All depends on the principles which direct them.

Napoleon Bonaparte

He who would learn to fly one day must first learn to stand and walk and run and climb and dance; one cannot fly into flying.

– Friedrich Nietzsche

Happiness is man's greatest aim in life. Tranquility and rationality are the cornerstones of happiness.

– Epicurus

10

Albert Einstein Quotes

Albert Einstein is best known for his theory of relativity and specifically mass–energy equivalence, $E = mc^2$. He received the 1921 Nobel Prize in Physics "for his services to Theoretical Physics, and especially for his discovery of the law of the photoelectric effect". In 1999, *Time magazine* named him the "Person of the Century". To many, the name "Einstein" has become synonymous with genius. The famous Einstein quotes given below will show how his intelligent mind and observations shine.

A man should look for what is, and not for what he thinks should be.

Any fool can make things bigger, more complex, and more violent. It takes a touch of genius—and a lot of courage—to move in the opposite direction.

Anyone who has never made a mistake has never tried anything new.

Everyone should be respected as an individual, but no one idolised.

Everything should be made as simple as possible, but not simpler.

Everything that can be counted does not necessarily count; everything that counts cannot necessarily be counted.

Few are those who see with their own eyes and feel with their own hearts.

Gravitation is not responsible for people falling in love.

Great spirits have always encountered violent opposition from mediocre minds.

If A is a success in life, then A equals x plus y plus z. Work is x; y is play; and z is keeping your mouth shut.

Imagination is everything. It is the preview of life's coming attractions.

Most people say that is it is the intellect which makes a great scientist. They are wrong: it is character.

No problem can be solved from the same level of consciousness that created it.

Once we accept our limits, we go beyond them.

Only a life lived for others is a life worthwhile.

Only two things are infinite, the universe and human stupidity, and I'm not sure about the former.

Our task must be to free ourselves by widening our circle of compassion to embrace all living creatures and the whole of nature and its beauty.

Strive not to be a success, but rather to be of value.

The distinction between the past, present and future is only a stubbornly persistent illusion.

The gift of fantasy has meant more to me than my talent or absorbing positive knowledge.

The high destiny of the individual is to serve rather than to rule.

The important thing is not to stop questioning. Curiosity has its own reason for existing.

The monotony and solitude of a quiet life stimulates the creative mind.

The most beautiful thing we can experience is the mysterious. It is the source of all true art and science.

The only real valuable thing is intuition.

The only reason for time is so that everything doesn't happen at once.

The pursuit of truth and beauty is a sphere of activity in which we are permitted to remain children all our lives.

There are only two ways to live your life. One is as though nothing is a miracle. The other is as though everything is a miracle.

When you sit with a nice girl for two hours, it seems like two minutes. When you sit on a hot stove for two minutes, it seems like two hours that's relativity.

11

Angel Quotes

Do you believe in angels? Are there are people in your life who's like angels to you? Here is a collection of beautiful angel quotes to inspire and lift your spirits up. You might open yourself up to receiving more miracles if you just believe, believe that you're not alone as this beautiful quote illustrates.

An angel is someone who helps you believe in miracles again. And that is a friend, lover, child.

— Author Unknown

Angels are messengers, but sometimes we misunderstand their language.

— Linda Solegato

Angels around us, angels beside us, angels within us. Angels are watching over you when times are good or stressed. Their wings wrap gently around you, whispering you are loved and blessed.

— Angel Blessing

Angels can fly because they carry no burdens.

— Eileen Elias Freeman

Angels can fly because they take themselves lightly.

— Gilbert K. Chesterton

Angels shine from without because their spirits are lit from within by the light of God.

— Eileen Elias Freeman

Be an angel to someone else whenever you can, as a way of thanking God for the help your angel has given you.

— Eileen Elias Freeman

Ever felt an angel's breath in the gentle breeze? A teardrop in the falling rain? Hear a whisper amongst the rustle of leaves? Or been kissed by a lone snowflake? Nature is an angel's favorite hiding place.

— Carrie Latet

Every blade of grass has its angel that bends over it and whispers, 'Grow, grow.'

— The Talmud

God not only sends special angels into our lives, but sometimes He even sends them back again if we forget to take notes the first time!

— Eileen Elias Freeman

If instead of a gem, or even a flower, we should cast the gift of a loving thought into the heart of a friend, that would be giving as the angels give.

— George MacDonald

It is only with the heart that one can see rightly; what is essential is invisible to the eye.

— Antoine De Saint-Exupery

Make yourself familiar with the angels and behold them frequently in spirit; for without being seen, they are present with you.

— St. Francis De Sales

Most people never have the opportunity to see an angel, or simply do not look well enough to see them walking among us. This, however does not mean they don't exist. Me, I'm one of the lucky few, not only have I seen an angel, I call her my best friend.

— Lori Corkum

Pay attention to your dreams—God's angels often speak directly to our hearts when we are asleep.

— Eileen Elias Freeman

Sometimes we are like an angel with one wing, and we necessarily need the other wing of a similar angel to keep flying.

– M. K. Soni

To see an angel, you must see another's soul.

To feel an angel, you must touch another's heart.

To hear an angel you must listen to both.

– Author Unknown

The golden moments in the stream of life rush past us and we see nothing but sand; the angels come to visit us, and we only know them when they are gone.

– George Eliot

The greatest achievement was at first and for a time a dream. The oak sleeps in the acorn, the bird waits in the egg, and in the highest vision of the soul a waking angel stirs. Dreams are the seedlings of realities.

– James Allen

The guardian angels of life sometimes fly so high as to be beyond our sight, but they are always looking down upon us.

– Jean Paul Richter

The reason angels can fly is because they take themselves lightly.

– G.K. Chesterton

These things I warmly wish for you Someone to love, some work to do, A bit o' sun, a bit o' cheer, And a guardian angel always near.

– Irish Blessings

12

Anger Quotes

Over the years, there have been many great quotes on anger. Listed below are some of the most famous anger quotes from some of the leaders in investing, business, and finance. Includes quotes about being angry, dealing with anger, and overcoming those that have been angered.

> Anyone can become angry. That is easy. But to be angry with the right person, to the right degree, at the right time, for the right purpose and in the right way... that is not easy.
>
> — ***Aristotle***

> If you are patient in one moment of anger, you will escape a hundred days of sorrow.
>
> — ***Chinese Proverb***

> Anger, if not restrained, is frequently more hurtful to us than the injury that provokes it.
>
> — ***Seneca***

> For every minute you remain angry, you give up sixty seconds of peace of mind.
>
> — ***Ralph Waldo Emerson***

> Holding on to anger is like grasping a hot coal with the intent of throwing it at someone else; you are the one who gets burned.
>
> — ***Buddha***

People who fly into a rage always make a bad landing.

— Will Rogers

Speak when you are angry and you will make the best speech you will ever regret.

— Ambrose Bierce

Consider how much more you often suffer from your anger and grief, than from those very things for which you are angry and grieved.

— Marcus Antonius

Do not teach your children never to be angry; teach them how to be angry.

— Lyman Abbott

How much more grievous are the consequences of anger than the causes of it.

— Marcus Aurelius

Two things a man should never be angry at: what he can help, and what he cannot help.

— Thomas Fuller

When a man is wrong and won't admit is, he always gets angry.

— Thomas Haliburton

There was never an angry man that thought his anger unjust.

— St. Francis De Sales

Anger is what makes a clear mind seem clouded.

— Kazi Shams

No man can think clearly when his fists are clenched.

— George Jean Nathan

Always write angry letters to your enemies. Never mail them.

James Fallows

Anger and intolerance are the enemies of correct understanding.

Mahatma Gandhi

Anger and jealousy can no more bear to lose sight of their objects than love.

George Eliot

Anger dwells only in the bosom of fools.

Albert Einstein

Anger is a killing thing: it kills the man who angers, for each rage leaves him less than he had been before—it takes something from him.

Louis L'Amour

Anger is a short madness.

Horace

Anger is a wind which blows out the lamp of the mind.

Robert Green Ingersoll

Anger is an acid that can do more harm to the vessel in which it is stored than to anything on which it is poured.

Mark Twain

Anger is one of the sinews of the soul.

Thomas Fuller

Anger, if not restrained, is frequently more hurtful to us than the injury that provokes it.

Lucius Annaeus Seneca

Bitterness is like cancer. It eats upon the host. But anger is like fire. It burns it all clean.

Maya Angelou

Expressing anger is a form of public littering.

Willard Gaylin

Fair peace becomes men; ferocious anger belongs to beasts.

Ovid

For every minute you remain angry, you give up sixty seconds of peace of mind.

Ralph Waldo Emerson

He who angers you conquers you.

Elizabeth Kenny

13

Aristotle Quotes

Dignity, humour, society, youth, misfortune—these are just a few of the subjects that Aristotle expressed his views on. Given below is a collection of famous Aristotle quotations. With trademark forthrightness, Aristotle presents compelling ideas about human existence.

The gods too are fond of a joke.

The only stable state is the one in which all men are equal before the law.

To give a satisfactory decision as to the truth it is necessary to be rather an arbitrator than a party to the dispute.

Young people are in a condition like permanent intoxication, because youth is sweet and they are growing.

Misfortune shows those who are not really friends.

Education is the best provision for old age.

Hope is a waking dream.

All human actions have one or more of these seven causes: chance, nature, compulsion, habit, reason, passion, and desire.

Dignity consists not in possessing honors, but in the consciousness that we deserve them.

Humour is the only test of gravity, and gravity of humor; for a subject which will not bear raillery is suspicious, and a jest which will not bear serious examination is false wit.

In the arena of human life the honors and rewards fall to those who show their good qualities.

It is the mark of an educated mind to be able to entertain a thought without accepting it.

Man perfected by society is the best of all animals; he is the most terrible of all when he lives without law, and without justice.

Men acquire a particular quality by constantly acting a particular way... you become just by performing just actions, temperate by performing temperate actions, brave by performing brave actions.

Liars when they speak the truth are not believed.

All men by nature desire knowledge.

It is possible to fail in many ways...while to succeed is possible only in one way.

14

Artist's Quotes

Here is a collection of famous artist quotes that inspire. Many of them are well-known artists of their days and in our times. Whether you are an artist or someone seeking to understand a bit more of these great artists, these quotes will inspire, motivate and encourage you.

Every child is an artist. The problem is how to remain an artist once he grows up.

— ***Pablo Picasso***

Everyone reaches a point in their life where they must either change or cease.

— ***Brett Whiteley***

Have no fear of perfection, you'll never reach it.

— ***Salvador Dali***

In our life there is a single colour, as on an artist's palette, which provides the meaning of life and art. It is the colour of love.

— ***Marc Chagall***

It took me four years to paint like Raphael, but a lifetime to paint like a child.

— ***Pablo Picasso***

It's on the strength of observation and reflection that one finds a way. So we must dig and delve unceasingly.

— ***Claude Monet***

No amount of skilful invention can replace the essential element of imagination.

— Edward Hopper

One can have no smaller or greater mastery than mastery of oneself.

— Leonardo da Vinci

One must from time to time attempt things that are beyond one's capacity.

— Auguste Renoir

Painting is an illusion, a piece of magic, so what you see is not what you see. I don't know what a painting is; who knows what sets off even the desire to paint? It might be things, thoughts, a memory, sensations, which have nothing to do directly with painting itself. They can come from anything and anywhere.

— Philip Guston

The artist is a receptacle for emotions that come from all over the place; from the sky, from the earth, from a scrap of paper, from a passing shape, from a spider's web.

— Pablo Picasso

The job of the artist is always to deepen the mystery.

— Francis Bacon

Those who do not want to imitate anything, produce nothing.

— Salvador Dali

To create one's own world in any of the arts takes courage.

— Georgia O'Keeffe

You have to systematically create confusion, it sets creativity free. Everything that is contradictory creates life.

— Salvador Dali

15

Attitude Quotes

Sometimes all it takes is a simple change in attitude to turn your life around. Here is a list of thought-provoking attitude quotes to highlight on this important quality. May these attitude quotes show you the power you hold in your hands to change your thoughts which in turn will change your circumstances.

A happy person is not a person in a certain set of circumstances, but rather a person with a certain set of attitudes.

— *Hugh Downs*

A non-doer is very often a critic-that is, someone who sits back and watches doers, and then waxes philosophically about how the doers are doing. It's easy to be a critic, but being a doer requires effort, risk, and change.

— *Dr. Wayne Dyer*

Become a possibilitarian. No matter how dark things seem to be or actually are, raise your sights and see possibilities—always see them, for they're always there.

— *Norman Vincent Peale*

Being a sex symbol has to do with an attitude, not looks. Most men think it's looks, most women know otherwise.

— *Kathleen Turner*

Could we change our attitude, we should not only see life differently, but life itself would come to be different.

— ***Katherine Mansfield***

Every thought is a seed. If you plant crab apples, don't count on harvesting Golden Delicious.

— ***Bill Meyer***

Happiness is an attitude. We either make ourselves miserable, or happy and strong. The amount of work is the same.

— ***Francesca Reigler***

Look at everything as though you were seeing it either for the first or last time.

— ***Betty Smith***

No life is so hard that you can't make it easier by the way you take it.

— ***Ellen Glasgow***

Nothing can stop the man with the right mental attitude from achieving his goal; nothing on earth can help the man with the wrong mental attitude.

— ***Thomas Jefferson***

Nothing is interesting if you're not interested.

— ***Helen MacInness***

Reach for the stars, even if you have to stand on a cactus.

— ***Susan Longacre***

Some days there won't be a song in your heart. Sing anyway.

— ***Emory Austin***

The greatest discovery of my generation is that human beings can alter their lives by altering their attitudes of mind.

— ***William James***

The world is full of cactus, but we don't have to sit on it.

— ***Will Foley***

There are no menial jobs, only menial attitudes.

— ***William J. Bennett***

There is little difference in people, but that little difference makes a big difference. The little difference is attitude. The big difference is whether it is positive or negative.

— ***W. Clement Stone***

Too many people miss the silver lining because they're expecting gold.

— ***Maurice Setter***

We all live under the same sky, but we don't all have the same horizon.

— ***Konrad Adenauer***

Wherever you go, no matter what the weather, always bring your own sunshine.

— ***Anthony J. D'Angelo***

Whenever you're in conflict with someone, there is one factor that can make the difference between damaging your relationship and deepening it. That factor is attitude.

— ***William James***

Your living is determined not so much by what life brings to you as by the attitude you bring to life; not so much by what happens to you as by the way your mind looks at what happens.

— ***Kahlil Gibran***

16

Art Quotes

Without art, the world would be a much less colourful and beautiful place. Everywhere we look, we could detect the art left by some inspired artists, but that appreciation would have to come from your own creative heart. These quotes uplift your spirits.

A work of art is a world in itself, reflecting senses and emotions of the artist's world.

— Hans Hofmann

A work of art is above all an adventure of the mind.

— Eugene Ionesco

All the arts we practice are apprenticeship. The big art is our life.

— M. C. Richards

Any authentic work of art must start an argument between the artist and his audience.

— Dame Rebecca West

Art enables us to find ourselves and lose ourselves at the same time.

— Thomas Merton

Art is a collaboration between God and the artist, and the less the artist does the better.

— Andre Gide

Art is a fruit that grows in man, like a fruit on a plant, or a child in its mother's womb.

— Jean Arp

Art is....a question mark in the minds of those who want to know what's happening.

— Aaron Howard

Art is born of the observation and investigation of nature.

— Cicero

Art is either plagiarism or revolution.

— Paul Gauguin

Art is everywhere, except it has to pass through a creative mind.

— Louise Nevelson

Art is indeed not the bread but the wine of life.

— Jean Paul Richter

Art is like a border of flowers along the course of civilisation.

— Lincoln Steffens

Art is not what you see, but what you make others see.

— Edgar Degas

Art is the desire of a man to express himself, to record the reactions of his personality to the world he lives in.

— Amy Lowell

Art is the only way to run away without leaving home.

— Twyla Tharp

Art is so wonderfully irrational, exuberantly pointless, but necessary all the same.

— Gunther Grass

Art is the imposing of a pattern on experience, and our aesthetic enjoyment is recognition of the pattern.

— Alfred North Whitehead

Art is the triumph over chaos.

— John Cheever

Art is when you hear a knocking from your soul—and you answer.

— Star Richés

Art, like morality, consists of drawing the line somewhere.

— G. K. Chesterton

As the sun colours flowers, so does art colour life.

— John Lubbock

Drawing is the honesty of the art. There is no possibility of cheating. It is either good or bad.

— Salvador Dali

Good art is not what it looks like, but what it does to us.

— Roy Adzak

Great art is the outward expression of an inner life in the artist.

— Edward Hopper

Great art picks up where nature ends.

— Marc Chagall

Life beats down and crushes the soul and art reminds you that you have one.

— Stella Adler

Simplicity is the essence of the great, the true, and the beautiful in art.

— George Sand

The aim of art is to represent not the outward appearance of things, but their inward significance.

— Aristotle

The art of art, the glory of expression and the sunshine of the light of letters, is simplicity.

— Walt Whitman

17

Autumn Quotes

The leaves are falling, announcing the arrival of autumn. Here is a collection of autumn quotes for your journaling, letters, scrapbook pages and greeting cards to friends and relatives. May these autumn quotes help to express your sentimental feelings and thoughts about this beautiful season.

All those golden autumn days the sky was full of wings. Wings beating low over the blue water of Silver Lake, wings beating high in the blue air far above it... bearing them all away to the green fields in the South.

— ***Laura Ingalls Wilder***

Autumn is a second spring where every leaf is a flower.

— ***Albert Camus***

Autumn is the eternal corrective. It is ripeness and colour and a time of maturity; but it is also breadth, and depth, and distance. What man can stand with autumn on a hilltop and fail to see the span of his world and the meaning of the rolling hills that reach to the far horizon?

— ***Hal Borland***

Bittersweet October. The mellow, messy, leaf-kicking, perfect pause between the opposing miseries of summer and winter.

— ***Carol Bishop Hipps***

Everyone must take time to sit and watch the leaves turn.

— Elizabeth Lawrence

For man, autumn is a time of harvest, of gathering together. For nature, it is a time of sowing, of scattering abroad.

— Edwin Way Teale

In the garden, Autumn is, indeed the crowning glory of the year, bringing us the fruition of months of thought and care and toil. And at no season, safe perhaps in Daffodil time, do we get such superb colour effects as from August to November.

— Rose G. Kingsley

October is a symphony of permanence and change.

— Bonaro W. Overstreet

The foliage has been losing its freshness through the month of August, and here and there a yellow leaf shows itself like the first gray hair amidst the locks of a beauty who has seen one season too many.

— Oliver Wendell Holmes

The lands are lit with all the autumn blaze of golden-rod, and everywhere the purple asters nod and bend and wave and flit.

— Helen Hunt

There is a harmony in autumn, and a luster in its sky, which through the summer is not heard or seen, as if it could not be, as if it had not been!

— Percy Bysshe Shelley

Winter is an etching, spring a watercolor, summer an oil painting and autumn a mosaic of them all.

— Stanley Horowitz

Youth is like spring, an over praised season more remarkable for biting winds than genial breezes. Autumn is the mellower season, and what we lose in flowers we more than gain in fruits.

— Samuel Butler

18

Baby Quotes

Having a baby is one of the most magical moments of your life. It practically turns your world upside down. The moment you hold your baby in your arms for the first time, you wonder how could such a tiny bundle of thing creates so much emotions within you. And you wonder if it's possible that you've actually brought such a tiny, beautiful being into this world. Here is a collection of adorable baby quotes will make you nod in agreement and break into quick smiles, because you know exactly what it's like to have a baby or babies in the house.

A baby is an inestimable blessing and bother.

— ***Mark Twain***

A baby is born with a need to be loved—and never outgrows it.

— ***Frank A. Clark***

A baby is God's opinion that the world should go on.

— ***Carl Sandburg***

A new baby is like the beginning of all things-wonder, hope, a dream of possibilities.

— ***Eda J. Le Shan***

A perfect example of minority rule is a baby in the house.

— ***Milwaukee Journal***

Babies are always more trouble than you thought—and more wonderful.

— *Charles Osgood*

Babies are bits of stardust, blown from the hand of God.

— *Barretto*

Babies are such a nice way to start people.

— *Don Herrold*

Babies control and bring up their families as much as they are controlled by them; in fact... the family brings up baby by being brought up by him.

— *Erik H. Erikson*

Babies need social interactions with loving adults who talk with them, listen to their babblings, name objects for them, and give them opportunities to explore their worlds.

— *Sandra Scarr*

Don't forget that compared to a grownup person every baby is a genius.

— *May Sarton*

Families with babies and families without are so sorry for each other.

— *Ed Howe*

Flowers are words which even a baby can understand.

— *Arthur C. Coxe*

Having a baby is like falling in love again, both with your husband and your child.

— *Tina Brown*

Having a child is surely the most beautifully irrational act that two people in love can commit.

— *Bill Cosby*

If your baby is "beautiful and perfect, never cries or fusses, sleeps on schedule and burps on demand, an angel all the time," you're the grandma."

— *Theresa Bloomingdale*

It is not a slight thing when those so fresh from God love us.

— ***Dickens***

Loving a baby is a circular business, a kind of feedback loop. The more you give the more you get and the more you get the more you feel like giving.

— ***Penelope Leach***

Making the decision to have a child is momentous. It is to decide forever to have your heart go walking around outside your body.

— ***Elizabeth Stone***

People who say they sleep like a baby usually don't have one.

— ***Leo J. Burke***

The smile that flickers on baby's lips when he sleeps- does anybody know where it was borne? Yes, there is a rumour that a young pale beam of a crescent moon touched the edge of a vanishing autumn cloud, and there the smile was first born...

— ***Rabindranath Tagore***

What good mothers and fathers instinctively feel like doing for their babies is usually best after all.

— ***Benjamin Spock***

When the first baby laughed for the first time, the laugh broke into a thousand pieces and they all went skipping about, and that was the beginning of fairies. And now when every new baby is born its first laugh becomes a fairy. So there ought to be.

— ***James Matthew Barrie***

19

Be Yourself Quotes

You are a very very special person. No one thing can sum you up. Sometimes it can be challenging to paint a picture of who's the inner person residing in you. To conform and fit into societal standards, you might have abandoned part of the real you. Here is some be yourself quotes to show you that you will be happier being the woman that you are, rather than pretending to be somebody else. These quotes may open your eyes to the marvels you hold within you.

A wise man never loses anything if he have himself.

— ***Michel de Montaigne, translated***

Almost all absurdity of conduct arises from the imitation of those whom we cannot resemble.

— ***Samuel Johnson***

Always be a first-rate version of yourself, instead of a second-rate version of somebody else.

— ***Judy Garland***

An unfulfilled vocation drains the color from a man's entire existence.

— ***Honoré de Balzac***

And remember, no matter where you go, there you are.

— ***Confucius***

Put a grain of boldness into everything you do.

— ***Baltasar Gracian***

At bottom every man knows well enough that he is a unique being, only once on this earth; and by no extraordinary chance will such a marvelously picturesque piece of diversity in unity as he is, ever be put together a second time.

— ***Friedrich Nietzsche***

Be what you are. This is the first step toward becoming better than you are.

— ***Julius Charles Hare***

Be who you are and say what you feel, because those who mind don't matter and those who matter don't mind.

— ***Dr. Seuss***

Every man is his own ancestor, and every man his own heir. He devises his own future, and he inherits his own past.

— ***H.F. Hedge***

Every time you don't follow your inner guidance, you feel a loss of energy, loss of power, a sense of spiritual deadness.

— ***Shakti Gawain***

How many cares one loses when one decides not to be something but to be someone.

— ***Gabrielle "Coco" Chanel***

It is better to be hated for what you are than to be loved for something you are not.

— ***Andre Gide***

It is only when we silent the blaring sounds of our daily existence that we can finally hear the whispers of truth that life reveals to us, as it stands knocking on the doorsteps of our hearts.

— ***K.T. Jong***

It is the chiefest point of happiness that a man is willing to be what he is.

— ***Desiderius Erasmus***

Most people are other people. Their thoughts are someone else's opinions, their lives a mimicry, their passions a quotation.

— Oscar Wilde

No creature is fully itself till it is, like the dandelion, opened in the bloom of pure relationship to the sun, the entire living cosmos.

— D.H. Lawrence

People often say that this or that person has not yet found himself. But the self is not something one finds, it is something one creates.

— Thomas Szasz

Take the time to come home to yourself every day.

— Robin Casarjean

The great majority of us are required to live a life of constant duplicity. Your health is bound to be affected if, day after day, you say the opposite of what you feel, if you grovel before what you dislike, and rejoice at what brings you nothing but misfortune.

— Boris Pasternak

The life of every man is a diary in which he means to write one story, and writes another.

— James Matthew Barrie

You have to leave the city of your comfort and go into the wilderness of your intuition. What you'll discover will be wonderful. What you'll discover is yourself.

— Alan Alda

You must have control of the authorship of your own destiny. The pen that writes your life story must be held in your own hand.

— Irene C. Kassorla

You must live your life from beginning to end: No one else can do it for you.

— Hopi saying

Your soul is all that you possess. Take it in hand and make something of it!

— Martin H. Fischer

20

Beauty Quotes

Beauty is not just confined to the looks of a beautiful young woman, beauty can come in the forms of nature, of people's souls, of art and words, and more. You can choose to see beauty everywhere, or you can choose to remain untouched. Here is a collection of beauty quotes to point out that you must carry beauty in your heart in order to reflect it outwards.

As we grow old, the beauty steals inward.

— ***Ralph Waldo Emerson***

Beauty is how you feel inside, and it reflects in your eyes. It is not something physical.

— ***Sophia Loren***

Beauty is in the eye of the beholder.

— ***Margaret Wolfe Hungerford***

Beauty is not in the face; beauty is a light in the heart.

— ***Kahlil Gibran***

Beauty of style and harmony and grace and good rhythm depend on Simplicity.

— ***Plato***

Beauty... when you look into a woman's eyes and see what is in her heart.

— ***Nate Dircks***

Everything has beauty, but not everyone sees it.

— Confucius

Everybody needs beauty as well as bread, places to play in and pray in, where nature may heal and give strength to body and soul.

— John Muir

It is amazing how complete is the delusion that beauty is goodness.

— Leo Tolstoy

Life is full of beauty. Notice it. Notice the bumble bee, the small child, and the smiling faces. Smell the rain, and feel the wind. Live your life to the fullest potential, and fight for your dreams.

— Ashley Smith

People are like stained-glass windows. They sparkle and shine when the sun is out, but when the darkness sets in their true beauty is revealed only if there is a light from within.

— Elisabeth Kubler-Ross

Some people, no matter how old they get, never lose their beauty—they merely move it from their faces into their hearts.

— Martin Buxbaum

Taking joy in living is a woman's best cosmetic.

— Rosalind Russell

That which is striking and beautiful is not always good, but that which is good is always beautiful.

— Ninon de L'Enclos

The best and most beautiful things in the world cannot be seen, nor touched... but are felt in the heart.

— Helen Keller

The future belongs to those who believe in the beauty of their dreams.

— Eleanor Roosevelt

The pursuit of truth and beauty is a sphere of activity in which we are permitted to remain children all our lives.

— Albert Einstein

The recipe for beauty is to have less illusion and more Soul, to retreat from the belief of pain or pleasure in the body into the unchanging calm and glorious freedom of spiritual harmony.

— ***Mary Baker Eddy***

The true beauty of a woman is her inherent ability to make better a man in every way.

— ***Don Williams, Jr***

There is certainly no absolute standard of beauty. That precisely is what makes its pursuit so interesting.

— ***John Kenneth Galbraith***

Think of all the beauty still left around you and be happy.

— ***Anne Frank***

Those who contemplate the beauty of the earth find reserves of strength that will endure as long as life lasts.

— ***Rachel Carson***

Though we travel the world over to find the beautiful, we must carry it with us or we find it not.

— ***Ralph Waldo Emerson***

We live in a wonderful world that is full of beauty, charm and adventure. There is no end to the adventures that we can have if only we seek them with our eyes open.

— ***Jawaharlal Nehru***

When you reach the heart of life you shall find beauty in all things, even in the eyes that are blind to beauty.

— ***Kahlil Gibran***

You cannot perceive beauty but with a serene mind.

— ***Henry David Thoreau***

Youth is happy because it has the capacity to see Beauty. Anyone who keeps the ability to see Beauty never grows old.

— ***Frank Kafka***

21

Believe Quotes

Here is a collection of believe quotes to bring you messages of the power of believing in yourself and in your goals. Many of these quotes will strengthen your beliefs in your choices, in your big dreams, in what you're doing. Some will make you question about believing others or the written rules.

Along with a strong belief in your own inner voice, you also need laser-like focus combined with unwavering determination.

— ***Larry Flynt***

Believe and act as if it were impossible to fail.

— ***Charles F. Kettering***

Believe deep down in your heart that you're destined to do great things.

— ***Joe Paterno***

Believe in yourself.. in all you can do.. and for you, the deals will start to work in your favour. You need to be open to such deals, and they will come, I assure you.

— ***Ivana Trump***

Believe it can be done. When you believe something can be done, really believe, your mind will find the ways to do it. Believing a solution paves the way to solution.

— ***David Joseph Schwartz***

Do not believe in anything simply because you have heard it. Do not believe in anything simply because it is spoken and rumoured by many. Do not believe in anything simply because it is found written in your religious books. Do not believe in anything merely on the authority of your teachers and elders. Do not believe in traditions because they have been handed down for many generations. But after observation and analysis, when you find that anything agrees with reason and is conducive to the good and benefit of one and all, then accept it and live up to it.

— ***Buddha***

Don't limit yourself. Many people limit themselves to what they think they can do. You can go as far as your mind lets you. What you believe, remember, you can achieve.

— ***Mary Kay Ash***

Every single life only becomes great when the individual sets upon a goal or goals which they really believe in, which they can really commit themselves to, which they can put their whole heart and soul into.

— ***Brian Tracy***

Every time you state what you want or believe, you're the first to hear it. It's a message to both you and others about what you think is possible. Don't put a ceiling on yourself.

— ***Oprah Winfrey***

Far away there in the sunshine are my highest aspirations. I may not reach them, but I can look up and see their beauty, believe in them, and try to follow where they lead.

— ***Louisa May Alcott***

If you believe in what you are doing, then let nothing hold you up in your work. Much of the best work of the world has been done against seeming impossibilities. The thing is to get the work done.

— ***Dale Carnegie***

If you believe you can, you probably can. If you believe you won't, you most assuredly won't. Belief is the ignition switch that gets you off the launching pad.

— *Denis Waitley*

Keep away from those who try to belittle your ambitions. Small people always do that, but the really great make you believe that you too can become great.

— *Mark Twain*

More than anything else, I believe it's our decisions, not the conditions of our lives, that determine our destiny.

— *Anthony Robbins*

Success means having the courage, the determination, and the will to become the person you believe you were meant to be.

— *George Sheehan*

The future belongs to those who believe in the beauty of their dreams.

— *Eleanor Roosevelt*

The only thing that stands between a man and what he wants from life is often merely the will to try it and the faith to believe that it is possible.

— *David Viscott*

What matters is not the idea a man holds, but the depth at which he holds it.

— *Ezra Pound*

Whatever you believe with feeling becomes your reality.

— *Brian Tracy*

Whatever you vividly imagine, ardently desire, sincerely believe, and enthusiastically act upon must inevitably come to pass.

— *Paul J. Meyer*

You can do it if you believe you can!

— *Napoleon Hill*

22

Bhagavad Gita Quotes

The *Bhagavad Gita* is one of the most important Hindu scriptures. It is revered as a sacred scripture of Hinduism, and considered as one of the most important philosophical classics of the world. Here is a collection of meaningful quotes from *Bhagavad Gita* that may open your eyes.

Better indeed is knowledge than mechanical practice. Better than knowledge is meditation. But better still is surrender of attachment to results, because there follows immediate peace.

Neither in this world nor elsewhere is there any happiness in store for him who always doubts.

Delusion arises from anger. The mind is bewildered by delusion. Reasoning is destroyed when the mind is bewildered. One falls down when reasoning is destroyed.

Man is made by his belief. As he believes, so he is.

The mind is restless and difficult to restrain, but it is subdued by practice.

Those who eat too much or eat too little, who sleep too much or sleep too little, will not succeed in meditation. But those who are temperate in eating and sleeping, work and recreation, will come to the end of sorrow through meditation.

The soul who meditates on the Self is content to serve the Self and rests satisfied within the Self; there remains nothing more for him to accomplish.

Fear Not. What is not real, never was and never will be. What is real, always was and cannot be destroyed.

Not by refraining from action does man attain freedom from action. Not by mere renunciation does he attain supreme perfection.

Action is greater than inaction. Perform therefore thy task in life. Even the life of the body could not be if there were no action.

When the sage climbs the heights of Yoga, he follows the path of work; but when he reaches the heights of Yoga, he is in the land of peace.

Whenever the mind unsteady and restless strays away from the spirit, let him ever and for ever lead it again to the spirit.

No work stains a man who is pure, who is in harmony, who is master of his life, whose soul is one with the soul of all.

23

Bible Quotes

The *Bible* is a book of faith and hope. Bible quotes calms the troubled mind and prayers bring solace to the soul. The Bible quotes given below are filled with wonderful words of wisdom and reassurance that God is always with us. Read these quotes from the *Bible* if you want to start out on a spiritual journey.

So will I sing praise unto thy name forever. That I may daily perform my vows.

— ***Psalm* 61:8**

Let every man have his own wife, and let every woman have her own husband. Let the husband render unto the wife due benevolence: and likewise also the wife unto the husband. The wife hath not the power of her own body, but the husband: and likewise also the husband hath not power of his own body, but the wife.

— ***Corinthians* 7:2-4**

There is neither Jew nor Greek, there is neither bond nor free, there is neither male nor female: for ye are all one in Christ.

— ***Galations* 3:28**

And Samuel came no more to see Saul until the day of his death: nevertheless Samuel mourned for Saul: and the LORD repented that he had made Saul king over Israel.

— ***Samuel* 15:35**

Except ye become as little children, ye will not enter the Kingdom of Heaven.

– Matthew 18:3

Cast your cares upon the Lord, for he cares about you.

– Peter 5:7

He covers the sky with clouds, he supplies the earth with rain, and maketh the grass grow on the hills.

– Psalms 147:8

Know ye not that ye are the temple of God and that the spirit of God dwelleth in you.

– Corinthians 3:16

A cheerful heart is good medicine, but a crushed spirit dries up the bones.

– Proverbs 17:22

Seek peace, and pursue it.

– Proverbs 34:14

My goodness, and my fortress; my high tower, and my deliverer; my shield, and he in whom I trust; who subdueth my people under me.

– Psalms 144:2

Everything is possible for him who believes.

– Mark 9:23

I know the plans I have for you, declares the Lord, plans to prosper you and not to harm you, plans to give you hope and a future.

– Jeremiah 29:11

Work hard and become a leader; be lazy and never succeed

– Proverbs 12:24

24

Birthday Quotes

Celebrating a birthday is exalting life and being glad for it. Here is a collection of beautiful birthday quotes. Pick out the most suitable quote on birthday, and use it in your greeting cards, letters to express your light-hearted, encouraging or warm wishes for that special someone.

A diplomat is a man who always remembers a woman's birthday but never remembers her age.

— Robert Frost

Age is not measured by years. Nature does not equally distribute energy. Some people are born old and tired while others are going strong at seventy.

— Dorothy Thompson

Age is strictly a case of mind over matter. If you don't mind, it doesn't matter.

— Jack Benny

And in the end, it's not the years in your life that count. It's the life in your years.

— Abraham Lincoln

At middle age the soul should be opening up like a rose, not closing up like a cabbage.

— John Andrew Holmes

At twenty years of age, the will reigns; at thirty, the wit; and at forty, the judgement.

— Benjamin Franklin

Birthdays are good for you. Statistics show that the people who have the most live the longest.

— Larry Lorenzoni

Few women admit their age. Few men act theirs.

— Anon

Forty is the old age of youth; fifty is the youth of old age.

— French proverb

Friendship is the shadow of the evening, which strengthens with the setting sun of life.

— Jean De La Fontaine

From birth to age eighteen, a girl needs good parents. From eighteen to thirty-five, she needs good looks. From thirty-five to fifty-five, she needs a good personality. From fifty-five on, she needs good cash.

— Sophie Tucker

It is better to wear out than to rust out.

— Bishop Richard Cumberland

Life begins at forty.

— W. B. Pitkin

Middle age is when you've met so many people that every new person you meet reminds you of someone else.

— Ogden Nash

Nature gives you the face you have at twenty, but it's up to you to merit the face you have at fifty.

— Coco Chanel

Some people, no matter how old they get, never lose their beauty–they merely move it from their faces into their hearts.

— Martin Buxbaum

The advantage of being eighty years old is that one has many people to love.

— Jean Renoir

The best way to remember your wife's birthday is to forget it once.

– H. V. Prochnow

The lovely thing about being forty is that you can appreciate twenty-five-year-old men.

– Colleen McCullough

The more you praise and celebrate your life, the more there is in life to celebrate.

– Oprah Winfrey

The older the fiddler, the sweeter the tune.

– English Proverb

The secret of staying young is to live honestly, eat slowly, and lie about your age.

– Lucille ball

Whatever with the past has gone, The best is always yet to come.

– Lucy Larcom

When I passed forty I dropped pretense, 'cause men like women who got some sense.

– Maya Angelou

When you turn thirty, a whole new thing happens: you see yourself acting like you parents.

– Blair Sabol

You grow up the day you have your first real laugh yourself.

– Ethel Barrymore

You make me chuckle when you say that you are no longer young, that you have turned twenty-four. A man is or may be young to after sixty, and not old before eighty.

– Oliver Wendell Holmes, Jr.

Youth is happy because it has the ability to see beauty. Anyone who keeps the ability to see beauty never grows old.

– Franz Kafka

25

Brother Quotes

Here is a collection of adorable brother quotes to bring out the different sides of emotions that our brothers invoke within us. Enjoy this list of loving brother quotes.

A brother is a friend provided by nature.

— Legouve Pere

Brothers and sisters are as close as hands and feet.

— Vietnamese Proverb

Brothers don't necessarily have to say anything to each other- they can sit in a room and be together and just be completely comfortable with each other.

— Leonardo Dicaprio

He aint heavy, he's my brother.

— Neil Diamond

He is my most beloved friend and my bitterest rival, my confidant and my betrayer, my sustainer and my dependent, and scariest of all, my equal.

— Gregg Levoy

Our brothers and sisters are there with us from the dawn of our personal stories to the inevitable dusk.

— Susan Scarf Merrell

Our siblings push buttons that cast us in roles we felt sure we had let go of long ago—the baby, the peacekeeper, the caretaker, the avoider.... It doesn't seem to matter how much time has elapsed or how far we've travelled.

– Jane Mersky Leder

Sometimes being a brother is even better than being a superhero.

– Marc Brown

The highlight of my childhood was making my brother laugh so hard that food came out his nose.

– Garrison Keillor

There is a destiny that makes us brothers, no one goes his way alone; all that we send into the lives of others, comes back into our own.

– Edwin Markham

There is a little boy inside the man who is my brother. Oh, how I hated that little boy. And how I love him too.

– Anna Quindlan

There's no other love like the love for a brother. There's no other love like the love from a brother.

– Astrid Alauda

To the outside world we all grow old. But not to brothers and sisters. We know each other as we always were. We know each other's hearts. We share private family jokes. We remember family feuds and secrets, family griefs and joys. We live outside the touch of time.

– Clara Ortega

We know one another's faults, virtues, catastrophes, mortifications, triumphs, rivalries, desires, and how long we can each hang by our hands to a bar. We have been banded together under pack codes and tribal laws.

– Rose Macaulay

When brothers agree, no fortress is so strong as their common life.

– Antisthenes

26

Boy Quotes

As the mother to your kids, your boys are always your favorite boys. They make you laugh, they make you marvel at their antics, they make you worry for them, yet you couldn't resist loving the boys in your life. They may be up to hundreds of mischiefs each day, they drive you crazy, yet at the end of each day, you couldn't help softly tucking them into bed and kissing them goodnight. Here is a collection of boy quotes that will show the fascinating sides of being a boy and more.

A boy becomes an adult three years before his parents think he does, and about two years after he thinks he does.

– Lewis B Hershey

A boy is a magical creature. You can lock him out of your workshop, but you can't lock him out of your heart. You can get him out of your study, but you can't get him out of your mind.

– Alan Beck

A boy's best friend is his mother.

– Joseph Stefano

A boy's story is the best that is ever told.

– Charles Dickens

A boy's will is the wind's will.

– Henry Wadsworth Longfellow

A fairly bright boy is far more intelligent and far better company than the average adult.

— ***John B.S. Haldane***

A small boy, mischievous to the imp degree.

— ***Rea Murtha***

A small son can charm himself into, and out of, most things.

— ***Jenny de Vries***

A treasure to a little boy does not consist of money, gems or jewellery. He will find far greater pleasure in the wonder of a rock, pebble, stick or beetle.

— ***Author Unknown***

Baseball is where boys practice being men and men practice being boys, and they get real good at it.

— ***Mary Cecile Leary***

Boys do not grow up gradually. They move forward in spurts like the hands of clocks in railway stations.

— ***Cyril Connolly***

Do not train boys to learning by force and harshness, but lead them by what amuses them, so that they may better discover the bent of their minds.

— ***Plato***

My mother had a great deal of trouble with me, but I think she enjoyed it.

— ***Mark Twain***

Nothing is so strong as gentleness; nothing so gentle as real strength.

— ***Francis De Sales***

Of all the animals, the boy is most unmanageable.

— ***Plato***

Only those who will risk going too far can possibly find out how far one can go.

— ***T.S. Eliot***

Sometimes being a brother is even better than being a superhero.

— Marc Brown

Sons are the anchors of a mother's life.

— Sophocles

Tall oaks from little acorns grow.

— David Everett

The sweetest roamer is a boy's young heart.

— George Edward Woodberry

There are three stages in a man's life: 'My Daddy can whip you Daddy.' 'Aw, Dad, you don't know anything.' 'My father used to say...'.

— Dwight McSmith

There comes a time in every rightly constructed boy's life when he has a raging desire to go somewhere and dig for hidden treasure.

— Mark Twain

There has never been a day when I have not been proud of you, I said to my Son though some days I'm louder about other stuff so it's easy to miss that.

— Brian Andreas

To become a real boy you must prove yourself brave, truthful, and unselfish.

— From "Pinnochio"

When I grow up I want to be a little boy.

— Joseph Heller

Wrapped around my son with only the knowledge of the words of the world and a quiet remembrance of watching before this all began.

— Brian Andreas

27

Buddha Quotes

Here is a beautiful collection of Buddha quotes to give you a glimpse of this great and remarkable spiritual teacher's teachings. Let the wisdom of the Buddha light up your journey of life.

Be a lamp unto yourself. Work out your liberation with diligence.

Be vigilant; guard your mind against negative thoughts.

Beings are owners of their action, heirs of their action.

Believe nothing, no matter where you read it, or who said it, no matter if I have said it, unless it agrees with your own reason and your own common sense.

Do not believe in anything simply because you have heard it. Do not believe in anything simply because it is spoken and rumoured by many. Do not believe in anything simply because it is found written in your religious books. Do not believe in anything merely on the authority of your teachers and elders. Do not believe in traditions because they have been handed down for many generations. But after observation and analysis, when you find that anything agrees with reason and is conducive to the good and benefit of one and all, then accept it and live up to it.

Fashion your life as a garland of beautiful deeds.

Hatred does not cease through hatred at any time. Hatred ceases through love. This is an unalterable law.

Have compassion for all beings, rich and poor alike; each has their suffering. Some suffer too much, others too little.

Holding on to anger is like grasping a hot coal with the intent of throwing it at someone else; you are the one who gets burned.

If we could see the miracle of a single flower clearly, our whole life would change.

Just as the great oceans have but one taste, the taste of salt, so too there is but one taste fundamental to all true teachings of the way, and this is the taste of freedom.

Let us rise up and be thankful, for if we didn't learn a lot today, at least we learned a little, and if we didn't learn a little, at least we didn't get sick, and if we got sick, at least we didn't die; so, let us all be thankful.

Let yourself be open and life will be easier. A spoon of salt in a glass of water makes the water undrinkable. A spoon of salt in a lake is almost unnoticed.

No one saves us but ourselves. No one can and no one may. We ourselves must walk the path.

Peace comes from within. Do not seek it without.

Teach this triple truth to all: A generous heart, kind speech, and a life of service and compassion are the things which renew humanity.

The secret of health for both mind and body is not to mourn for the past, worry about the future, or anticipate troubles, but to live in the present moment wisely and earnestly.

The way is not in the sky. The way is in the heart.

Thousands of candles can be lit from a single candle, and the life of the candle will not be shortened. Happiness never decreases by being shared.

Whatever words we utter should be chosen with care for people will hear them and be influenced by them for good or ill.

We are shaped by our thoughts; we become what we think. When the mind is pure, joy follows like a shadow that never leaves.

When you realise how perfect everything is you will tilt your head back and laugh at the sky.

You yourself, as much as anybody in the entire universe, deserve your love and affection.

Your work is to discover your work and then with all your heart to give yourself to it.

28

Business Quotes

Running a business is like riding on a roller coaster. Although it is fun and exciting, there will be times when you will be scared and feel powerless. During the bad times there isn't much you can do, other than to keep on pushing forward. So in that spirit, here are some quotes that will motivate you to push forward.

A budget tells us what we can't afford, but it doesn't keep us from buying it.

William Feather

A business that makes nothing but money is a poor business.

Henry Ford

A cardinal principle of Total Quality escapes too many managers: you cannot continuously improve interdependent systems and processes until you progressively perfect interdependent, interpersonal relationships.

Stephen Covey

About the time we can make the ends meet, somebody moves the ends.

Herbert Hoover

Airline travel is hours of boredom interrupted by moments of stark terror.

Al Boliska

All lasting business is built on friendship.

Alfred A. Montapert

Almost all quality improvement comes via simplification of design, manufacturing... layout, processes, and procedures.

Tom Peters

An advertising agency is 85 percent confusion and 15 percent commission.

Fred Allen

An economist is an expert who will know tomorrow why the things he predicted yesterday didn't happen today.

Laurence J. Peter

An economist's guess is liable to be as good as anybody else's.

Will Rogers

And while the law of competition may be sometimes hard for the individual, it is best for the race, because it ensures the survival of the fittest in every department.

Andrew Carnegie

Anyone who has lost track of time when using a computer knows the propensity to dream, the urge to make dreams come true and the tendency to miss lunch.

Tim Berners-Lee

As a small businessperson, you have no greater leverage than the truth.

John Greenleaf Whittier

Ask five economists and you'll get five different answers—six if one went to Harvard.

Edgar R. Fiedler

Blessed is he who has found his work; let him ask no other blessedness.

Thomas Carlyle

Business is a combination of war and sport.

Andre Maurois

Business, more than any other occupation, is a continual dealing with the future; it is a continual calculation, an instinctive exercise in foresight.

Henry R. Luce

Business, that's easily defined—it's other people's money.

Peter Drucker

By working faithfully eight hours a day you may eventually get to be boss and work twelve hours a day.

Robert Frost

Cannibals prefer those who have no spines.

Stanislaw Lem

Carpe per diem—seize the check.

Robin Williams

Corporation: An ingenious device for obtaining profit without individual responsibility.

Ambrose Bierce

Definition of a Statistician: A man who believes figures don't lie, but admits than under analysis some of them won't stand up either.

Evan Esar

Definition of Statistics: The science of producing unreliable facts from reliable figures.

Evan Esar

Do more than is required. What is the distance between someone who achieves their goals consistently and those who spend their lives and careers merely following? The extra mile.

Gary Ryan Blair

Do not trust people. They are capable of greatness.

Stanislaw Lem

Don't gamble; take all your savings and buy some good stock and hold it till it goes up, then sell it. If it don't go up, don't "uy it.

Will Rogers

Don't let your ego get too close to your position, so that if your position gets shot down, your ego doesn't go with it.

Colin Powell

Don't simply retire from something; have something to retire to.

Harry Emerson Fosdick

Don't worry about people stealing your ideas. If your ideas are any good, you'll have to ram them down people's throats.

Howard Aiken

Economic depression cannot be cured by legislative action or executive pronouncement. Economic wounds must be healed by the action of the cells of the economic body—the producers and consumers themselves.

Herbert Hoover

Effective leadership is putting first things first. Effective management is discipline, carrying it out.

Stephen Covey

Effort only fully releases its reward after a person refuses to quit.

Napoleon Hill

Employees make the best dates. You don't have to pick them up and they're always tax-deductible.

Andy Warhol

Every day I get up and look through the Forbes list of the richest people in America. If I'm not there, I go to work.

Robert Orben

29

Change Quotes

If the stimulus is the need to change, the typical response is to reject that need. We prefer to reject change rather than embrace it. Change forces us to explore new turf. When there is no change, things are familiar, and hence there is a feeling of security. Change is unsettling. But change can add an exciting twist to a mundane life. If you like a fast paced life, full of twists and turns, read some provoking change quotes that remind you of the benefits of change.

Everything changes, nothing remains without change.

– Buddha

Be the change you want to see in the world.

– Mahatma Gandhi

Change is not made without inconvenience, even from worse to better.

– Richard Hooker

If you don't create change, change will create you.

– Anonymous

Change is the only constant.

– Proverb

The first step toward change is awareness. The second step is acceptance.

– Nathaniel Branden

There is nothing wrong with change, if it is in the right direction.

— Winston Churchill

When you're finished changing, you're finished.

— Benjamin Franklin

Change your thoughts and you change your world.

— Norman Vincent Peale

If you don't like the way the world is, you change it. You have an obligation to change it. You just do it one step at a time.

— Marian Wright Edelman

Change is inevitable—except from a vending machine.

— Robert C. Gallagher

People underestimate their capacity for change. There is never a right time to do a difficult thing. A leader's job is to help people have vision of their potential.

— John Porter

Change alone is eternal, perpetual, immortal.

— Arthur Schopenhauer

None of us knows what the next change is going to be, what unexpected opportunity is just around the corner, waiting a few months or a few years to change all the tenor of our lives.

— Kathleen Norris

Technological change is like an axe in the hands of a pathological criminal.

— Albert Einstein

All things change; nothing perishes.

— Ovid

We know what we are, but know not what we may be.

— William Shakespeare

The need for change bulldozed road down the centre of my mind.

— Maya Angelou

30

Character Quotes

Your character will speak so loudly about you, that it overpowers what you may try to convince others in words. So wherever you go, and whoever you are with, ultimately given time, your character will shine through as it's the foundation of who you are. Here is a thought-provoking collection of quotes about character.

> A person will worship something, have no doubt about that. We may think our tribute is paid in secret in the dark recesses of our hearts, but it will out. That which dominates our imaginations and our thoughts will determine our lives, and our character. Therefore, it behooves us to be careful what we worship, for what we are worshipping we are becoming.
>
> – *Ralph Waldo Emerson*

> Any fool can criticise, condemn, and complain but it takes character and self-control to be understanding and forgiving.
>
> – *Dale Carnegie*

> Character cannot be developed in ease and quiet. Only through experience of trial and suffering can the soul be strengthened, vision cleared, ambition inspired, and success achieved.
>
> – *Helen Keller*

> Character contributes to beauty. It fortifies a woman as her youth fades. A mode of conduct, a standard of

courage, discipline, fortitude, and integrity can do a great deal to make a woman beautiful.

— Author Unknown

Character is doing the right thing when nobody's looking. There are too many people who think that the only thing that's right is to get by, and the only thing that's wrong is to get caught.

— J. C. Watts

Character, in the long run, is the decisive factor in the life of an individual and of nations alike.

— Theodore Roosevelt

Character is simply habit long continued.

— Plutarch

Character—the willingness to accept responsibility for one's own life—is the source from which self-respect springs.

— Joan Didion

Character isn't something you were born with and can't change, like your fingerprints. It's something you weren't born with and must take responsibility for forming.

— Jim Rohn

Character, not circumstance, makes the person.

— Booker T. Washington

I have no regrets in my life. I think that everything happens to you for a reason. The hard times that you go through build character, making you a much stronger person.

— Rita Mero

No change of circumstances can repair a defect of character.

— Ralph Waldo Emerson

Parents can only give good advice or put them on the right paths, but the final forming of a person's character lies in their own hands.

— Anne Frank

People do not seem to realise that their opinion of the world is also a confession of character.

— ***Ralph Waldo Emerson***

People grow through experience if they meet life honestly and courageously. This is how character is built.

— ***Eleanor Roosevelt***

Personality can open doors, but only character can keep them open.

— ***Elmer G. Letterman***

Sow a thought, and you reap an act; Sow an act, and you reap a habit; Sow a habit, and you reap a character; Sow a character, and you reap a destiny.

— ***Charles Reade***

Talents are best nurtured in solitude, but character is best formed in the stormy billows of the world.

— ***Johann Wolfgang von Goethe***

The best index to a person's character is (a) how he treats people who can't do him any good, and (b) how he treats people who can't fight back.

— ***Abigail Van Buren***

The measure of a man's real character is what he would do if he knew he would never be found out.

— ***Thomas Babington Macaulay***

The true test of character is not how much we know how to do, but how we behave when we don't know what to do.

— ***John W. Holt, Jr.***

You can easily judge the character of a man by how he treats those who can do nothing for him.

— ***Johann Wolfgang von Goethe***

You cannot dream yourself into a character; you must hammer and forge yourself one.

— ***James A. Froude***

31

Children Quotes

Children are little people of today and adults of tomorrow. And these children quotations will show you that your kids have lots to offer you too. Once you have children in your house, it seems like you're leading a completely different life from before. Here is a delightful collection of children quotes that will share with you some tips about bringing up young children. Kid quotes also highlight on what you can learn from your little people.

A child can ask questions that a wise man cannot answer.

— *Author Unknown*

All the flowers of all the tomorrows are in the seeds of today.

— *Indian Proverb*

All kids are gifted. Some just open their packages earlier than others.

— *Michael Carr*

All kids need is a little help, a little hope and somebody who believes in them.

— *Earvin Magic Johnson*

Blessed be childhood, which brings down something of heaven into the midst of our rough earthliness.

— *Henri Frederic Amiel*

Bliss was it in that dawn to be alive. But to be young was very heaven!

— *William Wordsworth*

Cherish your dreams. Follow your passions. They are the guiding hands of your heart.

— *Flavia*

Childhood, catching our imagination when it is fresh and tender, never lets go of us.

— *J. B. Priestly*

Childhood is measured out by sounds and smells and sights, before the dark hour of reason grows.

— *John Betjeman*

Childhood is the world of miracle and wonder... as if creation rose, bathed in the light, out of the darkness, utterly new and fresh and astonishing. The end of childhood is when things cease to astonish us.

— *Eugene Ionesco*

Childhood, whose very happiness is love.

— *Letitia Landon*

Children are likely to live up to what you believe in them.

— *Ladybird Johnson*

Children are the living messages we send to a time we will not see.

— *John W. Whitehead*

Children are natural Zen masters; their world is brand new in each and every moment.

— *John Bradshaw*

Children are unpredictable. You never know what inconsistency they're going to catch you in next.

— *Franklin P. Jones*

Children make you want to start life over.

— *Muhammad Ali*

Children run wildly, breathlessly... facing the wind...absorbing its speed.

— *Author Unknown*

Every child comes with the message that God is not yet discouraged of man.

— *Rabindranath Tagore*

Every child is an artist. The problem is how to remain an artist once he grows up.

— *Pablo Picasso*

My best creation is my children.

— *Diane Von Furstenberg*

Stop trying to perfect your child, but keep trying to perfect your relationship with him.

— *Dr. Henker*

There are no seven wonders of the world in the eyes of a child. There are seven million.

— *Walt Streightiff*

There is no substitute for books in the life of a child.

— *Mary Ellen Chase*

There's nothing that can help you understand your beliefs more than trying to explain them to an inquisitive child.

— *Frank A. Clark*

You are worried about seeing him spend his early years in doing nothing. What! Is it nothing to be happy? Nothing to skip, play, and run around all day long? Never in his life will he be so busy again.

— *Jean-Jacques Rousseau*

You can learn many things from children. How much patience you have, for instance.

— *Franklin P. Jones*

Your children will see what you're all about by what you live rather than what you say.

— *Wayne Dyer*

32

Christmas Quotes

Christmas is the magical holiday season of the year. What do you think of when you think of Christmas—family gatherings, hectic buying of gifts, posting of Christmas cards, crazy wrapping up of gifts? Here is a collection of Christmas quotes to bring up feelings of goodwill, love, poignancy and wonderful longings.

Christmas, children, is not a date. It is a state of mind.

— ***Mary Ellen Chase***

Christmas Eve was a night of song that wrapped itself about you like a shawl. But it warmed more than your body. It warmed your heart... filled it, too, with a melody that would last forever.

— ***Bess Streeter Aldrich***

Christmas is forever, not for just one day, for loving, sharing, giving, are not to put away like bells and lights and tinsel, in some box upon a shelf. The good you do for others is good you do yourself.

— ***Norman W. Brooks***

Christmas is the gentlest, loveliest festival of the revolving year—and yet, for all that, when it speaks, its voice has strong authority.

— ***W.J. Cameron***

Christmas is most truly Christmas when we celebrate it by giving the light of love to those who need it most.

— ***Ruth Carter Stapleton***

Christmas is the season for kindling the fire of hospitality in the hall, the genial flame of charity in the heart.

— ***Washington Irving***

Christmas, my child, is love in action. Every time we love, every time we give, it's Christmas.

— ***Dale Evans Rogers***

It is Christmas in the heart that puts Christmas in the air.

— ***W.T. Ellis***

Never worry about the size of your Christmas tree. In the eyes of children, they are all 30 feet tall.

— ***Larry Wilde***

Peace on earth will come to stay,
When we live Christmas every day.

— ***Helen Steiner Rice***

The best of all gifts around any Christmas tree: the presence of a happy family all wrapped up in each other.

— ***Burton Hillis***

Until one feels the spirit of Christmas, there is no Christmas. All else is outward display--so much tinsel and decorations. For it isn't the holly, it isn't the snow. It isn't the tree not the firelight's glow. It's the warmth that comes to the hearts of men when the Christmas spirit returns again.

— ***Author Unknown***

What is Christmas? It is tenderness for the past, courage for the present, hope for the future. It is a fervent wish that every cup may overflow with blessings rich and eternal, and that every path may lead to peace.

— ***Agnes M. Pharo***

33

Computers Quotes

Computer is an electronic device that has become essential for the day to day work execution in all the big places of work, like companies, schools, etc. a computer has become the lifeline of everybody these days. This device has eased the work of people, which was otherwise done manually in the primitive times. The computer quotes give us an insight to the advantages and uses of computers. They tell us about how were these built and the motives behind their being invented, which all people were responsible for their inventions.

A computer once beat me at chess, but it was no match for me at kick boxing.

Emo Philips

Bill Gates is the Pope of the personal computer industry. He decides who's going to build.

Larry Ellison

Computer science is no more about computers than astronomy is about telescopes.

Edsger Dijkstra

Computers are magnificent tools for the realisation of our dreams, but no machine can replace the human spark of spirit, compassion, love, and understanding.

Louis Gerstner

Computers are useless. They can only give you answer.

Pablo Picasso

Computers make it easier to do a lot of things, but most of the things they make it easier to do don't need to be done.

Andy Rooney

Computing is not about computers any more. It is about living.

Nicholas Negroponte

Data is not information, information is not knowledge, knowledge is not understanding, understanding is not wisdom.

Clifford Stoll

Home computers are being called upon to perform many new functions, including the consumption of homework formerly eaten by the dog.

Doug Larson

I am not the only person who uses his computer mainly for the purpose of diddling with his computer.

Dave Barry

I do not fear computers. I fear the lack of them.

Isaac Asimov

I think computer viruses should count as life. I think it says something about human nature that the only form of life we have created so far is purely destructive. We've created life in our own image.

Stephen Hawking

I think it's fair to say that personal computers have become the most empowering tool we've ever created. They're tools of communication, they're tools of creativity, and they can be shaped by their user.

Bill Gates

Never trust a computer you can't throw out a window.

Steve Wozniak

Part of the inhumanity of the computer is that, once it is competently programmed and working smoothly, it is completely honest.

Isaac Asimov

People think computers will keep them from making mistakes. They're wrong. With computers you make mistakes faster.

Adam Osborne

Supercomputers will achieve one human brain capacity by 2010, and personal computers will do so by about 2020.

Ray Kurzweil

The computer is a moron.

Peter Drucker

The Internet is not just one thing, it's a collection of things—of numerous communications networks that all speak the same digital language.

Jim Clark

The real danger is not that computers will begin to think like men, but that men will begin to think like computers.

Sydney J. Harris

Think? Why think! We have computers to do that for us.

Jean Rostand

To err is human—and to blame it on a computer is even more so.

Robert Orben

Treat your password like your toothbrush. Don't let anybody else use it, and get a new one every six months.

Clifford Stoll

Why is it drug addicts and computer afficionados are both called users?

Clifford Stoll

34

Courage Quotes

You will always need courage to deal with your life situations, love, family and work. You need courage to live your life the way you want to. Most of all, you need courage to be what you are. Here is an inspiring collection of quotes about courage to motivate and encourage you.

All art requires courage.

— ***Anne Tucker***

Anyone can give up, it's the easiest thing in the world to do. But to hold it together when everyone else would understand if you fell apart, that's true strength.

— ***Author Unknown***

Be brave. Take risks. Nothing can substitute experience.

— ***Paulo Coelho***

Being deeply loved by someone gives you strength while loving someone deeply gives you courage.

— ***Lao Tse***

Courage doesn't always roar. Sometimes courage is the little voice at the end of the day that says I'll try again tomorrow.

— ***Mary Anne Radmacher***

Courage is being afraid but going on anyhow.

— ***Dan Rather***

Courage is being scared to death... and saddling up anyway.

— John Wayne

Courage is doing what you're afraid to do. There can be no courage unless you're scared.

— Edward Vernon Rickenbacker

Courage is going from failure to failure without losing enthusiasm.

— Winston Churchill

Courage is never to let your actions be influenced by your fears.

— Arthur Koestler

Courage is not the absence of fear, but rather the judgement that something else is more important than fear.

— Ambrose Redmoon

Courage is not the absence of fear, it is taking a step forward when you are afraid.

— Ken McGrath

Courage is the discovery that you may not win, and trying when you know you can lose.

— Tom Krause

Courage is what it takes to stand up and speak; courage is also what it takes to sit down and listen.

— Winston Churchill

Have the courage to say no. Have the courage to face the truth. Do the right thing because it is right. These are the magic keys to living your life with integrity.

— W. Clement Stone

History, despite its wrenching pain, cannot be unlived, but if faced with courage, need not be lived again.

— Maya Angelou

It takes a lot of courage to show your dreams to someone else.

— Erma Bombeck

Many of our fears are tissue paper-thin, and a single courageous step would carry us through them.

— Brendan Francis

One life is all we have and we live it as we believe in living it. But to sacrifice what you are and to live without belief, that is a fate more terrible than dying.

— Joan of Arc

Pain nourishes courage. You can't be brave if you've only had wonderful things happen to you.

— Mary Tyler Moore

The greatest test of courage on the earth is to bear defeat without losing heart.

— R. G. Ingersoll

The important thing is this: To be able at any moment to sacrifice what we are for what we could become.

— Charles DuBois

To dare is to lose one's footing momentarily. To not dare is to lose oneself.

— Soren Kierkegaard

We could never learn to be brave and patient if there were only joy in the world.

— Helen Keller

Yesterday I dared to struggle. Today I dare to win.

— Bernadette Devlin

You don't develop courage by being happy in your relationships everyday. You develop it by surviving difficult times and challenging adversity.

— Epicurus

You gain strength, courage, and confidence by every experience in which you really stop to look fear in the face. You must do the thing which you think you cannot do.

— Eleanor Roosevelt

35

Creativity Quotes

Here is an invaluable list of motivational and inspirational quotations on creativity. These creativity quotes are fantastic at encouraging others to take a more creative outlook on life. Understand their wisdom and use them to motivate yourself and others.

Another word for creativity is courage.

-- George Prince

Creativity comes from trust. Trust your instincts. And never hope more than you work.

– Rita Mae Brown

Creativity involves breaking out of established patterns in order to look at things in a different way.

– Edward de Bono

Creativity is a drug I cannot live without.

– Cecil B. DeMille

Creativity is a type of learning process where the teacher and pupil are located in the same individual.

– Arthur Koestler

Creativity is inventing, experimenting, growing, taking risks, breaking rules, making mistakes, and having fun.

– Mary Lou Cook

Creativity is the ability to see relationships where none exist.

– Thomas Disch

Creativity is the power to connect the seemingly unconnected.

— *William Plomer*

Creativity—like human life itself—begins in darkness.

— *Julia Cameron*

Creativity requires the courage to let go of certainties.

— *Erich Fromm*

Don't let anyone rob you of your imagination, your creativity, or your curiosity. It's your place in the world; it's your life. Go on and do all you can with it, and make it the life you want to live.

— *Mae Jemison*

Don't think. Thinking is the enemy of creativity. It's self-conscious, and anything self-conscious is lousy. You can't try to do things. You simply must do things.

— *Ray Bradbury*

Enthusiasm is excitement with inspiration, motivation, and a pinch of creativity.

— *Bo Bennett*

Happiness is not in the mere possession of money; it lies in the joy of achievement, in the thrill of creative effort.

— *Franklin D. Roosevelt*

Imagination is the beginning of creation. You imagine what you desire, you will what you imagine and at last you create what you will.

— *George Bernard Shaw*

I never feel age... If you have creative work, you don't have age or time.

— *Louise Nevelson*

It is better to create than to be learned, creating is the true essence of life.

— *Barthold Georg Niebuhr*

To live a creative life, we must lose our fear of being wrong.

— *Joseph Chilton Pearce*

It's hard for corporations to understand that creativity is not just about succeeding. It's about experimenting and discovering.

— Gordon Mackenzie

Making the simple complicated is commonplace; making the complicated simple, awesomely simple, that's creativity.

— Charles Mingus

Sometimes creativity just means the daily work of helping others to see a problem in a different way.

— Joseph Badaracco

The ability to relate and to connect, sometimes in odd and yet striking fashion, lies at the very heart of any creative use of the mind, no matter in what field or discipline.

— George J. Seidel

The creative person is willing to live with ambiguity. He doesn't need problems solved immediately and can afford to wait for the right ideas.

— Abe Tannenbaum

The problem is never how to get new, innovative thoughts into your mind, but how to get old ones out. Every mind is a building filled with archaic furniture. Clean out a corner of your mind and creativity will instantly fill it.

— Dee Hock

There are two ways of being creative. One can sing and dance. Or one can create an environment in which singers and dancers flourish.

— Warren G. Bennis

There's room for everybody on the planet to be creative and conscious if you are your own person. If you're trying to be like somebody else, then there is isn't.

— Tori Amos

Uncertainty and mystery are energies of life. Don't let them scare you unduly, for they keep boredom at bay and spark creativity.

— R. I. Fitzhenry

36

Dalai Lama Quotes

Often refer to as His Holiness, the 14th Dalai Lama of Tibet is both the head of state and the spiritual leader of Tibet. Read through these Dalai Lama quotes and you will realise that love, kindness, compassion, peace and happiness are often mentioned in his teachings.

An affectionate disposition not only makes the mind more peaceful and calm, but it affects our body in a positive way too.

Basically we are all the same human beings with the same potential to be a good human being or a bad human being... The important thing is to realise the positive side and try to increase that; realise the negative side and try to reduce. That's the way.

Be kind whenever possible...It is always possible.

Compassion and tolerance are not a sign of weakness, but a sign of strength.

First one must change. I first watch myself, check myself, then expect changes from others.

Happiness is not something ready made. It comes from your own actions.

In the practice of tolerance, one's enemy is the best teacher.

Human beings are of such nature that they should have not only material facilities but spiritual sustenance as well. Without spiritual sustenance, it is difficult to get and maintain peace of mind.

I believe all suffering is caused by ignorance. People inflict pain on others in the selfish pursuit of their happiness or satisfaction. Yet true happiness comes from a sense of peace and contentment, which in turn must be achieved through the cultivation of altruism, of love and compassion, and elimination of ignorance, selfishness, and greed.

I believe that the very purpose of life is to be happy. From the very core of our being, we desire contentment. In my own limited experience I have found that the more we care for the happiness of others, the greater is our own sense of well-being.

I feel that the essence of spiritual practice is your attitude toward others. When you have a pure, sincere motivation, then you have right attitude toward others based on kindness, compassion, love and respect.

I truly believe that individuals can make a difference in society. Since periods of change such as the present one come so rarely in human history, it is up to each of us to make the best use of our time to help create a happier world.

If the love within your mind is lost and you see other beings as enemies, then no matter how much knowledge or education or material comfort you have, only suffering and confusion will ensue.

If there is love, there is hope to have real families, real brotherhood, real equanimity, real peace. If the love within your mind is lost, if you continue to see other beings as enemies, then no matter how much knowledge or education you have, no matter how much material progress is made, only suffering and confusion will ensue.

If you want others to be happy, practice compassion. If you want to be happy, practice compassion.

It is easy to point out the mistakes of others, while it is hard to admit one's own mistakes. A man broadcasts the sins of others without thinking, but he hides his own sins as a gambler hides his extra dice.

Love and compassion are necessities, not luxuries. Without them humanity cannot survive.

Love and kindness are the very basis of society. If we lose these feelings, society will face tremendous difficulties; the survival of humanity will be endangered.

My religion is very simple. My religion is kindness.

My message is the practice of compassion, love and kindness. Compassion can be put into practice if one recognises the fact that every human being is a member of humanity and the human family regardless of differences in religion, culture, colour and creed. Deep down there is no difference.

Old friends pass away, new friends appear. It is just like the days. An old day passes, a new day arrives. The important thing is to make it meaningful: a meaningful friend—or a meaningful day.

Our prime purpose in this life is to help others. And if you can't help them, at least don't hurt them.

Share your knowledge. It's a way to achieve immortality.

Sleep is the best meditation.

Spend some time alone every day.

The purpose of our lives is to be happy.

The realisation that we are all basically the same human beings who seek happiness and try to avoid suffering is very helpful in developing a sense of brotherhood and sisterhood; a warm feeling of love and compassion for others.

The roots of all goodness lie in the soil of appreciation for goodness.

This is my simple religion. There is no need for temples; no need for complicated philosophy. Our own brain, our own heart is our temple; the philosophy is kindness.

Today, more than ever before, life must be characterised by a sense of Universal responsibility, not only nation to nation and human to human, but also human to other forms of life.

We can live without religion and meditation, but we cannot survive without human affection.

When we are young and again when we are old, we depend heavily on the affection of others. Between these stages we usually feel that we can do everything without help from others and that other people's affection is simply not important. But at this stage I think it is very important to keep deep human affection.

When you think everything is someone else's fault, you will suffer a lot. When you realise that everything springs only from yourself, you will learn both peace and joy. Pride leads to violence and evil. The truly good gaze upon everything with love and understanding.

Whether one believes in a religion or not, and whether one believes in rebirth or not, there isn't anyone who doesn't appreciate kindness and compassion.

With the realisation of one's own potential and self-confidence in one's ability, one can build a better world.

37

Daughter Quotes

Whether your daughter is still a little girl or a grown-up woman, she'll always remain as your girl and will hold a special place in your heart. It is probably from your daughter that you learned about the sweetness and spice of little girls. It's also from her that you learned about patience and forgiveness, as she stretched your tolerance with the sulky attitude of a teenage girl. Here is a collection of loving daughter quotes to gently remind yourself and her of how precious your daughter is to you. These beautiful and inspiring quotes about daughters will speak of your love for your girl.

A daughter is a bundle of firsts that excite and delight, giggles that come from deep inside and are always contagious, everything wonderful and precious and your love for her knows no bounds.

— ***Barbara Cage***

A daughter is a miracle that never ceases to be miraculous...full of beauty and forever beautiful...loving and caring and truly amazing.

— ***Deanna Beisser***

A daughter is a treasure—and a cause of sleeplessness.

— ***Ben Sirach***

A daughter is one of the most beautiful gifts this world has to give.

— ***Laurel Atherton***

A mother's treasure is her daughter.

— Catherine Pulsifer

A son is a son till he takes him a wife, a daughter is a daughter all of her life.

—Irish Saying

Certain is it that there is no kind of affection so purely angelic as of a father to a daughter. In love to our wives there is desire; to our sons, ambition; but to our daughters there is something which there are no words to express.

— Joseph Addison

Daughter are angles sent from above to fill our heart with unending love.

— J. Lee

Never grow a wishbone, daughter, where you backbone ought to be.

— Clementine Paddleford

Oh my son's my son till he gets him a wife, but my daughter's my daughter all her life.

— Dinah Maria Mulock Craik

Our daughters are the most precious of our treasures, the dearest possessions of our homes and the objects of our most watchful love.

— Margaret E. Sangster

To a father growing old nothing is dearer than a daughter.

— Euripides

There's something like a line of gold thread running through a man's words when he talks to his daughter, and gradually over the years it gets to be long enough for you to pick up in your hands and weave into a cloth that feels like love itself.

— John Gregory Brown

What I wanted most for my daughter was that she be able to soar confidently in her own sky, whatever that may be.

— Helen Claes

38

Dog Quotes

Here is a collection that will make you eye your doggy friend with puppy love, make you laugh, and some will just make you think. Some of these paw-perfect quotes inspire. Some are just plain funny. Whether it's inspirational or simply funny, you are bound to find a great quote that express your loving feelings about your favourite pet in the world.

A dog is one of the remaining reasons why some people can be persuaded to go for a walk.

— ***O.A. Battista***

Bulldogs are adorable, with faces like toads that have been sat on.

— ***Colette***

Buy a pup and your money will buy love unflinching.

— ***Rudyard Kipling***

Dogs are not our whole life, but they make our lives whole.

— ***Roger Caras***

Dogs are our link to paradise. They don't know evil or jealousy or discontent. To sit with a dog on a hillside on a glorious afternoon is to be back in Eden, where doing nothing was not boring—it was peace.

— ***Milan Kundera***

Dogs feel very strongly that they should always go with you in the car, in case the need should arise for them to bark violently at nothing right in your ear.

— Dave Barry

Dogs have given us their absolute all. We are the centre of their universe. We are the focus of their love and faith and trust. They serve us in return for scraps. It is without a doubt the best deal man has ever made.

— Roger Caras

Dogs' lives are too short. Their only fault, really.

— Agnes Sligh Turnbull

Every dog must have his day.

— Jonathan Swift

Happiness is a warm puppy.

— Charles M. Schulz

He is your friend, your partner, your defender, your dog. You are his life, his love, his leader. He will be yours, faithful and true, to the last beat of his heart. You owe it to him to be worthy of such devotion.

— Author Unknown

I have a dog and sometimes I'll be the littlest kid with my dog and marvel at his ears and his nose and how he looks at me. If he died, I'd bawl like a baby.

— Aaron Eckhart

I love a dog. He does nothing for political reasons.

— Will Rogers

I think dogs are the most amazing creatures; they give unconditional love. For me they are the role model for being alive.

— Gilda Radner

I wonder if other dogs think poodles are members of a weird religious cult.

— Rita Rudner

If dogs could talk it would take a lot of the fun out of owning one.

— Andy Rooney

If you are a dog and your owner suggests that you wear a sweater... suggest that he wear a tail.

— Fran Lebowitz

If you get to thinkin' you're a person of some influence, try orderin' somebody else's dog around.

— Cowboy Wisdom

If you pick up a starving dog and make him prosperous, he will not bite you; that is the principal difference between a dog and a man.

— Mark Twain

I've seen a look in dogs' eyes, a quickly vanishing look of amazed contempt, and I am convinced that basically dogs think humans are nuts.

— John Steinbeck

Labradors [are] lousy watchdogs. They usually bark when there is a stranger about, but it is an expression of unmitigated joy at the chance to meet somebody new, not a warning.

— Norman Strung

My dog is worried about the economy because Alpo is up to 99 cents a can. That's almost $7.00 in dog money.

— Joe Weinstein

My goal in life is to be as good of a person my dog already thinks I am.

— Author Unknown

My husband and I are either going to buy a dog or have a child. We can't decide whether to ruin our carpets or ruin our lives.

— Rita Rudner

No matter how little money and how few possessions you own, having a dog makes you rich.

— Louis Sabin

No one appreciates the very special genius of your conversation as the dog does.

— Christopher Morley

No symphony orchestra ever played music like a two-year-old girl laughing with a puppy.

— Bern Williams

One reason a dog can be such a comfort when you're feeling blue is that he doesn't try to find out why.

— Author Unknown

Puppies are nature's remedy for feeling unloved, plus numerous other ailments of life.

— Richard Allan Palm

The dog was created specially for children. He is the god of frolic.

— Henry Ward Beecher

The great pleasure of a dog is that you may make a fool of yourself with him and not only will he not scold you, but he will make a fool of himself too.

— Samuel Butler

There is no psychiatrist in the world like a puppy licking your face.

— Ben Williams

They [dogs] never talk about themselves but listen to you while you talk about yourself, and keep up an appearance of being interested in the conversation.

— Jerome K. Jerome

Things that upset a terrier may pass virtually unnoticed by a Great Dane.

— Smiley Blanton

We long for an affection altogether ignorant of our faults. Heaven has accorded this to us in the uncritical canine attachment.

— George Eliot

Whoever said you can't buy happiness forgot little puppies.

— Gene Hill

39

Dream Quotes

Whatever ways that your dreams come to you, dreams are important. They are like hopes for a future that we envision and hold on tightly in our hearts. Be careful to weed out negative thoughts and to fertilise your dreams with visualisation, persistence and action. We have to have a dream before our dreams can come true. We have to know what it is that we want out of life so that we know when we arrive. This collection of inspirational dream quotes provide you a source of encouragement and enthusiasm as you work towards making your dreams come true.

> A dream is your creative vision for your life in the future. You must break out of your current comfort zone and become comfortable with the unfamiliar and the unknown.
>
> — *Denis Waitley*

> A goal is a dream with a deadline.
>
> — *Napoleon Hill*

> A man's dreams are an index to his greatness.
>
> — *Zadok Rabinwitz*

> A rock pile ceases to be a rock pile the moment a single man contemplates it, bearing within him the image of a cathedral.
>
> — *Antoine De Saint-Exupery*

Be careful what you water your dreams with. Water them with worry and fear and you will produce weeds that choke the life from your dream. Water them with optimism and solutions and you will cultivate success. Always be on the lookout for ways to turn a problem into an opportunity for success. Always be on the lookout for ways to nurture your dream.

— Lao Tzu

Dream as if you'll live forever... live as if you'll die today.

— James Dean

Dream what you want to dream; go where you want to go; be what you want to be, because you have only one life and one chance to do all the things you want to do.

— Author Unknown

Dreams are free, so free your dreams.

— Astrid Alauda

Dreams are renewable. No matter what our age or condition, there are still untapped possibilities within us and new beauty waiting to be born.

— Dale E. Turner

Every great dream begins with a dreamer. Always remember, you have within you the strength, the patience, and the passion to reach for the stars to change the world.

— Harriet Tubman

For my part I know nothing with any certainty, but the sight of the stars makes me dream.

— Vincent van Gogh

Happy are those who dream dreams and are ready to pay the price to make them come true.

— Leon Joseph Cardinal Suenens

How do you go from where you are to where you want to be? I think you have to have an enthusiasm for life. You have to have a dream, a goal, and you have to be willing to work for it.

— Jim Valvano

If one dream should fall and break into a thousand pieces, never be afraid to pick one of those pieces up and begin again.

— ***Flavia Weedn***

If the dream is big enough the facts don't matter.

— ***Dexter Yager***

If you have a dream, give it a chance to happen.

— ***Richard M. DeVos***

If you're still hanging onto a dead dream of yesterday, laying flowers on its grave by the hour, you cannot be planting the seeds for a new dream to grow today.

— ***Joyce Chapman***

Life is never easy for those who dream.

— ***Robert James Waller***

Only as high as I reach can I grow, only as far as I seek can I go, only as deep as I look can I see, only as much as I dream can I be.

— ***Karen Ravn***

People who soar are those who refuse to sit back, sigh and wish things would change. They neither complain of their lot nor passively dream of some distant ship coming in. Rather, they visualise in their minds that they are not quitters; they will not allow life's circumstances to push them down and hold them under.

— ***Author Unknown***

Reach high, for stars lie hidden in your soul. Dream deep, for every dream precedes the goal.

— ***Pamela Vaull Starr***

Some men see things as they are and ask why. Others dream things that never were and ask why not.

— ***George Bernard Shaw***

There will always be dreams grander or humbler than your own, but there will never be a dream exactly like your own... for you are unique and more wondrous than you know!

— ***Linda Staten***

Those who cherish a beautiful vision, a lofty ideal in their hearts, will one day realise it.

— *James Allen*

Twenty years from now you will be more disappointed by the things that you didn't do than by the ones you did do. So throw off the bowlines. Sail away from the safe harbor. Catch the trade winds in your sails. Explore. Dream. Discover.

— *Mark Twain*

We are the music makers and we are the dreamers of dreams...

— *Arthur O'Shaughnessy*

We grow great by dreams. All big men are dreamers. They see things in the soft haze of a spring day or in the red fire of a long winter's evening. Some of us let these great dreams die, but others nourish and protect them; nurse them through bad days till they bring them to the sunshine and light which comes always to those who sincerely hope that their dreams will come true.

— *Woodrow Wilson*

Whatever you do, or dream you can, begin it. Boldness has genius and power and magic in it.

— *Johann Wolfgang von Goethe*

You are never given a dream without also being given the power to make it true. You may have to work for it, however.

— *Richard Bach*

You are never too old to set another goal or to dream a new dream.

— *C.S. Lewis*

You block your dream when you allow your fear to grow bigger than your faith.

— *Mary Manin Morrissey*

You can't just sit there and wait for people to give you that golden dream. You've got to get out there and make it happen for yourself.

— *Diana Ross*

You have to dream before your dreams can come true.

— Abdul Kalam

You have to have a dream so you can get up in the morning.

— Billy Wilder

You see things; and you say, 'Why?' But I dream things that never were; and I say, 'Why not?'

— George Bernard Shaw

You're in the midst of a war: a battle between the limits of a crowd seeking the surrender of your dreams, and the power of your true vision to create and contribute. It is a fight between those who will tell you what you cannot do, and that part of you that knows/ and has always known/ that we are more than our environment; and that a dream, backed by an unrelenting will to attain it, is truly a reality with an imminent arrival.

— Anthony Robbins

40

Education Quotes

When you choose to educate with a heart full of love, what you can do will reach far beyond what you can ever imagine. Enjoy these education quotes and educational quotes.

> A word as to the education of the heart. We don't believe that this can be imparted through books; it can only be imparted through the loving touch of the teacher.
>
> — ***Cesar Chavez***

> Children require guidance and sympathy far more than instruction.
>
> — ***Annie Sullivan***

> Do not train children to learning by force and harshness, but direct them to it by what amuses their minds, so that you may be better able to discover with accuracy the peculiar bent of the genius of each.
>
> — ***Plato***

> Educate the heart. Let us have good men.
>
> — ***Hiram Powers***

> Education costs money, but then so does ignorance.
>
> — ***Sir Claus Moser***

> Education is not filling a bucket, but lighting a fire.
>
> — ***William Butler Yeats***

> Education is for improving the lives of others and for leaving your community and world better than you found it.
>
> — ***Marian Wright Edelman***

Education is not a product: mark, diploma, job, money in that order; it is a process, a never ending one.

— ***Bel Kaufman***

Education would be so much more effective if its purpose were to ensure that by the time they leave school every boy and girl should know how much they don't know, and be imbued with a lifelong desire to know it.

— ***Sir William Haley***

Formal education will make you a living; self-education will make you a fortune.

— ***Jim Rohn***

Give me six hours to chop down a tree and I will spend the first four sharpening the axe.

— ***Abraham Lincoln***

In times of change, learners inherit the Earth, while the learned find themselves beautifully equipped to deal with a world that no longer exists.

— ***Eric Hoffer***

It is a thousand times better to have common sense without education than to have education without common sense.

— ***Robert Green Ingersoll***

One mark of a great educator is the ability to lead students out to new places where even the educator has never been.

— ***Thomas Groome***

The aim of education should be to teach us rather how to think, than what to think—rather to improve our minds, so as to enable us to think for ourselves, than to load the memory with thoughts of other men.

— ***Bill Beattic***

The educator must believe in the potential power of his pupil, and he must employ all his art in seeking to bring his pupil to experience this power.

— ***Alfred Adler***

The kids in our classroom are infinitely more significant than the subject matter we teach.

— ***Meladee McCarty***

The man who can make hard things easy is the educator.

— Ralph Waldo Emerson

The mind is not a vessel to be filled but a fire to be kindled.

— Plutarch

The most important function of education at any level is to develop the personality of the individual and the significance of his life to himself and to others.

— Grayson Kirk

The one real object of education is to have a man in the condition of continually asking questions.

— Bishop Creighton

The principal goal of education is to create men who are capable of doing new things, not simply of repeating what other generations have done—men who are creative, inventive and discoverers.

— Jean Piaget

The whole art of teaching is only the art of awakening the natural curiosity of young minds for the purpose of satisfying it afterwards.

— Anatole France

We cannot hold a torch to light another's path without brightening our own.

— Ben Sweetland

What sculpture is to a block of marble, education is to the human soul.

— Joseph Addison

We have a hunger of the mind which asks for knowledge of all around us, and the more we gain, the more is our desire; the more we see, the more we are capable of seeing.

— Maria Mitchell

What is important is to keep learning, to enjoy challenge, and to tolerate ambiguity. In the end there are no certain answers.

— Martina Horner

41

Helen Keller Quotes

Helen Keller has been a truly inspiring icon. Having lost sight and hearing ability at a very young age, Helen learned to grapple with life's small and big struggles. Her indomitable spirit saw her through her handicap. This collection of Helen Keller quotes will speak of the ideas of this world-famous and remarkable deafblind American author, activist, lecturer and woman.

Although the world is full of suffering, it is full also of the overcoming of it.

Character cannot be developed in ease and quiet. Only through experience of trial and suffering can the soul be strengthened, ambition inspired, and success achieved.

I am only one, but still I am one. I cannot do everything, but still I can do something; and because I cannot do everything, I will not refuse to do something that I can do.

I long to accomplish a great and noble task, but it is my chief duty to accomplish small tasks as if they were great and noble.

Life is either a daring adventure or nothing at all. Security is mostly a superstition. It does not exist in nature.

One can never consent to creep when one feels an impulse to soar.

The best and most beautiful things in the world cannot be seen or even touched. They must be felt within the heart.

One can never consent to creep when one feels an impulse to soar.

What we have once enjoyed we can never lose. All that we love deeply becomes a part of us.

When one door of happiness closes, another opens; but often we look so long at the closed door that we do not see the one which has been opened for us.

When we do the best that we can, we never know what miracle is wrought in our life, or in the life of another.

It is wonderful how much time good people spend fighting the devil. If they would only expend the same amount of energy loving their fellow men, the devil would die in his own tracks of ennui.

Keep your face to the sunshine and you cannot see the shadows.

Believe. No pessimist ever discovered the secrets of the stars, or sailed to an uncharted land, or opened a new heaven to the human spirit.

It is for us to pray not for tasks equal to our powers, but for powers equal to our tasks, to go forward with a great desire forever beating at the door of our hearts as we travel toward our distant goal.

One can never consent to creep when one feels an impulse to soar.

Optimism is the faith that leads to achievement. Nothing can be done without hope and confidence.

Walking with a friend in the dark is better than walking alone in the light.

We can do anything we want if we stick to it long enough.

We would never learn to be brave and patient if there were only joy in the world.

Character cannot be developed in ease and quiet. Only through experiences of trial and suffering can the soul be strengthened, vision cleared, ambition inspired and success achieved.

Faith is the strength by which a shattered world shall emerge into the light.

Relationships are like Rome – difficult to start out, incredible during the prosperity of the 'golden age', and unbearable during the fall. Then, a new kingdom will come along and the whole process will repeat itself until you come across a kingdom like Egypt... that thrives, and continues to flourish. This kingdom will become your best friend, your soul mate, and your love.

42

Family Quotes

These meaningful quotes about families will touch, inspire and move you. They are fabulous for your cards, scrapbooks, letters or as reminders about the importance of families.

A family is a unit composed not only of children but of men, women, an occasional animal, and the common cold.

— Ogden Nash

A happy family is but an earlier heaven.

— John Bowring

A man can't make a place for himself in the sun if he keeps taking refuge under the family tree.

— Helen Keller

A man travels the world over in search of what he needs, and returns home to find it.

— George Moore

At the end of the day, a loving family should find everything forgivable.

— Mark V. Olsen and Will Sheffer

Bringing up a family should be an adventure, not an anxious discipline in which everybody is constantly graded for performance.

— Milton R. Saperstein

Call it a clan, call it a network, call it a tribe, call it a family: Whatever you call it, whoever you are, you need one.

— Jane Howard

Families are the compass that guide us. They are the inspiration to reach great heights, and our comfort when we occasionally falter.

— Brad Henry

Family: A social unit where the father is concerned with parking space, the children with outer space, and the mother with closet space.

— Evan Esar

Family faces are magic mirrors looking at people who belong to us, we see the past, present, and future.

— Gail Lumet Buckley

Family is just accident.... They don't mean to get on your nerves. They don't even mean to be your family, they just are.

— Marsha Norman

Happiness is having a large, loving, caring, close-knit family in another city.

— George Burns

Home is the place where boys and girls first learn how to limit their wishes, abide by rules, and consider the rights and needs of others.

— Sidonie Gruenberg

Important families are like potatoes. The best parts are underground.

— Francis Bacon

In each family a story is playing itself out, and each family's story embodies its hope and despair.

— Auguste Napier

In every conceivable manner, the family is link to our past, bridge to our future.

— Alex Haley

In every dispute between parent and child, both cannot be right, but they may be, and usually are, both wrong. It is this situation which gives family life its peculiar hysterical charm.

— *Isaac Rosenfeld*

In family life, love is the oil that eases friction, the cement that binds closer together, and the music that brings harmony.

— *Eva Burrows*

Like all the best families, we have our share of eccentricities, of impetuous and wayward youngsters and of family disagreements.

— *Elizabeth II*

No matter what you've done for yourself or for humanity, if you can't look back on having given love and attention to your own family, what have you really accomplished?

— *Elbert Hubbard*

Other things may change us, but we start and end with the family.

— *Anthony Brandt*

The family is one of nature's masterpieces.

— *George Santayana*

The family—that dear octopus from whose tentacles we never quite escape, nor, in our inmost hearts, ever quite wish to.

— *Dodie Smith*

The family. We were a strange little band of characters trudging through life sharing diseases and toothpaste, coveting one another's desserts, hiding shampoo, borrowing money, locking each other out of our rooms, inflicting pain and kissing to heal it in the same instant, loving, laughing, defending, and trying to figure out the common thread that bound us all together.

— *Erma Bombeck*

The family you come from isn't as important as the family you're going to have.

— ***Ring Lardner***

The only rock I know that stays steady, the only institution I know that works is the family.

— ***Lee Iacocca***

To us, family means putting your arms around each other and being there.

— ***Barbara Bush***

The happiest moments of my life have been the few which I have passed at home in the bosom of my family.

— ***Thomas Jefferson***

We cannot destroy kindred: our chains stretch a little sometimes, but they never break.

— ***Marquise de Sévigné***

What greater thing is there for human souls than to feel that they are joined for life—to be with each other in silent unspeakable memories.

— ***George Eliot***

When you look at your life, the greatest happinesses are family happinesses.

— ***Joyce Brothers***

You don't choose your family. They are God's gift to you, as you are to them.

— ***Desmond Tutu***

Your family and your love must be cultivated like a garden. Time, effort, and imagination must be summoned constantly to keep any relationship flourishing and growing.

— ***Jim Rohn***

43

Failure Quotes

Everyone fails at some point in her life. Success tastes much sweeter when we know what failure tasted like. We appreciate success better when we have known failure before. Here is a collection of failure quotes to put things into perspective and encourage us to set forth courageously again.

A garden is always a series of losses set against a few triumphs, like life itself.

— *May Sarton*

A man may fall many times, but he won't be a failure until he says that someone pushed him.

— *Elmer G. Letterman*

An inventor fails 999 times, and if he succeeds once, he's in. He treats his failures simply as practice shots.

— *Charles F. Kettering*

But there is suffering in life, and there are defeats. No one can avoid them. But it's better to lose some of the battles in the struggles for your dreams than to be defeated without ever knowing what you're fighting for.

— *Paulo Coelho*

Do not waste yourself in rejection, nor bark against the bad, but chant the beauty of the good.

— *Ralph Waldo Emerson*

Failure is a detour, not a dead-end street.

— Zig Ziglar

Failure is instructive. The person who really thinks learns quite as much from his failures as from his successes.

— John Dewey

Failure is nature's plan to prepare you for great responsibilities.

— Napoleon Hill

Failure is not a single, cataclysmic event. You don't fail overnight. Instead, failure is a few errors in judgement, repeated every day.

— Jim Rohn

Failure is only a temporary change in direction to set you straight for your next success.

— Denis Waitley

Failure is simply the opportunity to begin again, this time more intelligently.

— Henry Ford

Failure is success if we learn from it.

— Malcolm S. Forbes

Failure is the tuition you pay for success.

— Walter Brunell

Failure should be our teacher, not our undertaker. Failure is delay, not defeat. It is a temporary detour, not a dead end. Failure is something we can avoid only by saying nothing, doing nothing, and being nothing.

— Denis Waitley

Failures are finger posts on the road to achievement.

— C.S. Lewis

I cannot give you the formula for success, but I can give you the formula for failure: which is: Try to please everybody.

— Herbert B. Swope

I have not failed. I've just found 10,000 ways that won't work.

— Thomas Alva Edison

If there exists no possibility of failure, then victory is meaningless.

— Robert H. Schuller

If you are not big enough to lose, you are not big enough to win.

— Walter Reuther

If you have made mistakes, there is always another chance for you. You may have a fresh start any moment you choose, for this thing we call 'failure' is not the falling down, but the staying down.

— Mary Pickford

It is a mistake to suppose that men succeed through success; they much oftener succeed through failures. Precept, study, advice, and example could never have taught them so well as failure has done.

— Samuel Smiles

It is not the critic who counts, not the man who points out how the strong man stumbled, or where the doer of deeds could have done better. The credit belongs to the man who is actually in the arena, whose face is marred by dust and sweat and blood, who strives valiantly, who errs and comes short again and again, who knows the great enthusiasms, the great devotions, and spends himself in a worthy cause, who at best knows achievement and who at the worst if he fails at least fails while daring greatly so that his place shall never be with those cold and timid souls who know neither victory nor defeat.

— Theodore Roosevelt

It is on our failures that we base a new and different and better success.

— Havelock Ellis

Keep on beginning and failing. Each time you fail, start all over again, and you will grow stronger until you have accomplished a purpose—not the one you began with perhaps, but one you'll be glad to remember.

— ***Anne Sullivan***

My reputation grows with every failure.

— ***George Bernard Shaw***

My will shall shape the future. Whether I fail or succeed shall be no man's doing but my own. I am the force; I can clear any obstacle before me or I can be lost in the maze. My choice; my responsibility; win or lose, only I hold the key to my destiny.

— ***Elaine Maxwell***

Never confuse a single defeat with a final defeat.

— ***F. Scott Fitzgerald***

Notice the difference between what happens when a man says to himself, "I have failed three times," and what happens when he says, "I am a failure."

— ***S.I. Hayakawa***

Only those who dare to fail greatly can ever achieve greatly.

— ***Robert F. Kennedy***

Our greatest glory is not in never falling, but in rising every time we fall.

— ***Confucius***

Remember the two benefits of failure. First, if you do fail, you learn what doesn't work; and second, the failure gives you the opportunity to try a new approach.

— ***Roger Von Oech***

The greatest barrier to success is the fear of failure.

— ***Sven Goran Eriksson***

There are no failures—just experiences and your reactions to them.

— ***Tom Krause***

There is something good in all seeming failures. You are not to see that now. Time will reveal it. Be patient.

— Swami Sivananda

Think like a queen. A queen is not afraid to fail. Failure is another stepping stone to greatness.

— Oprah Winfrey

We seem to gain wisdom more readily through our failures than through our successes. We always think of failure as the antithesis of success, but it isn't. Success often lies just the other side of failure.

— Leo F. Buscaglia

What would you do if you knew you could not fail?

— Robert H. Schuller

When defeat comes, accept it as a signal that your plans are not sound, rebuild those plans, and set sail once more toward your coveted goal.

— Napoleon Hill

When we begin to take our failures non-seriously, it means we are ceasing to be afraid of them. It is immense importance to learn to laugh at ourselves.

— Katherine Mansfield

You always pass failure on your way to success.

— Mickey Rooney

44

Faith Quotes

In the road of everyday living, there's bound to be many uncertainties and doubts arising. In times of troubles, what keep your mind clear and your heart hopeful? Faith might be the answer. Faith can take you over doubts. It can be a faithful companion while you walk the path only you can walk. Faith in yourself and your path will bring illumination to the darkness of fears, doubts and uncertainties. Here is a collection of faith quotes to shine light on the importance of having faith in your daily living.

As your faith is strengthened you will find that there is no longer the need to have a sense of control, that things will flow as they will, and that you will flow with them, to your great delight and benefit.

— ***Emmanuel Teney***

Be faithful in small things because it is in them that your strength lies.

— ***Mother Teresa***

Be faithful to that which exists nowhere but in yourself—and thus make yourself indispensable.

— ***Andre Gide***

Do not put your faith in what statistics say until you have carefully considered what they do not say.

— ***William W. Watt***

Exercise of faith will be the safest where there is a clear determination summarily to reject all that is contrary to truth and love.

– Mahatma Gandhi

Every tomorrow has two handles. We can take hold of it with the handle of anxiety or the handle of faith.

– Henry Ward Beecher

Faith is a knowledge within the heart, beyond the reach of proof.

– Kahlil Gibran

Faith is an oasis in the heart which can never be reached by the caravan of thinking.

– Kahlil Gibran

Faith is a passionate intuition.

– William Wordsworth

Faith is a process of leaping into the abyss not on the basis of any certainty about "where" we shall land, but rather on the belief that we "shall" land.

– Carter Heyward

Faith is courage; it is creative while despair is always destructive.

– David S. Muzzey

Faith is like electricity. You can't see it, but you can see the light.

– Author Unknown

Faith is not a delicate flower which would wither away under the slightest stormy weather.

– Mahatma Gandhi

Faith is not something to grasp, it is a state to grow into.

– Mahatma Gandhi

Faith is not trying to believe something regardless of the evidence; faith is daring something regardless of the consequences.

– Sherwood Eddy

Faith is reason grown courageous.

— *Sherwood Eddy*

Faith is taking the first step even when you don't see the whole staircase.

— *Martin Luther King, Jr.*

Faith is the bird that feels the light and sings when the dawn is still dark.

— *Rabindranath Tagore*

Faith is the strength by which a shattered world shall emerge into the light.

— *Helen Keller*

Faith is to believe what you do not see; the reward of this faith is to see what you believe.

— *Saint Augustine*

Faith is the art of holding on to things your reason has once accepted in spite of your changing moods.

— *C.S. Lewis*

Faith makes the discords of the present the harmonies of the future.

— *Robert Collyer*

Faith means belief in something concerning which doubt is theoretically possible.

— *William James*

Faith means living with uncertainty—feeling your way through life, letting your heart guide you like a lantern in the dark.

— *Dan Millman*

Fear can keep us up all night long, but faith makes one fine pillow.

— *Philip Gulley*

Fear clogs; Faith liberates.

— *Elbert Hubbard*

If you think you can win, you can win. Faith is necessary to victory.

— *William Hazlitt*

He who has faith has... an inward reservoir of courage, hope, confidence, calmness, and assuring trust that all will come out well—even though to the world it may appear to come out most badly.

— B.C. Forbes

If you can't have faith in what is held up to you for faith, you must find things to believe in yourself, for a life without faith in something is too narrow a space to live.

— George E Woodberry

It's faith in something and enthusiasm for something that makes a life worth living.

— Oliver Wendell Holmes

Keep your dreams alive. Understand to achieve anything requires faith and belief in yourself, vision, hard work, determination, and dedication. Remember all things are possible for those who believe.

— Gail Devers

Living without faith is like driving in a fog.

— Proverb

On a long journey of human life, faith is the best of companions; it is the best refreshment on the journey; and it is the greatest property.

— Buddha

Only the person who has faith in himself is able to be faithful to others.

— Erich Fromm

Optimism is the faith that leads to achievement. Nothing can be done without hope and confidence.

— Helen Keller

Scepticism is the beginning of Faith.

— Oscar Wilde

Talk unbelief, and you will have unbelief; but talk faith, and you will have faith. According to the seed sown will be the harvest.

— Ellen G. White

The keys to patience are acceptance and faith. Accept things as they are, and look realistically at the world around you. Have faith in yourself and in the direction you have chosen.

— Ralph Marston

To one who has faith, no explanation is necessary. To one without faith, no explanation is possible.

— St. Thomas Aquinas

When you walk to the edge of all the light you have and take that first step into the darkness of the unknown, you must believe that one of two things will happen: There will be something solid for you to stand upon, or, you will be taught how to fly.

— Patrick Overton

When you put faith, hope and love together, you can raise positive kids in a negative world.

— Zig Ziglar

Where there is hatred, let me sow love. Where there is injury, pardon. Where there is doubt, faith.

— St Francis of Assisi

You block your dream when you allow your fear to grow bigger than your faith.

— Mary Manin Morrissey

45

Farewell Quotes

Certain farewells can be harder than others. When we are to part with friends and know in our hearts that somewhere in the future that we will meet again, the farewell can be bittersweet. But if we are to part for an uncertain period of time from a loved one, the farewell will take on a different dimension. If you are looking for some inspirational farewell quotes to put into your farewell speech or cards, do read about these farewell quotes.

> Don't be dismayed at goodbyes, a farewell is necessary before you can meet again and meeting again, after moments or lifetimes, is certain for those who are friends.
>
> — ***Richard Bach***

> Don't cry because it's over. Smile because it happened.
>
> — ***Dr. Seuss***

> Every parting is a form of death, as every reunion is a type of heaven.
>
> — ***Tryon Edwards***

> Goodbyes are not forever.
> Goodbyes are not the end.
> They simply mean I'll miss you
> Until we meet again!
>
> — ***Author Unknown***

Happy trails to you, until we meet again.
Some trails are happy ones,
Others are blue.
It's the way you ride the trail that counts,
Here's a happy one for you.

— Dale Evans

Man's feelings are always purest and most glowing in the hour of meeting and of farewell.

— Jean Paul Richter

No distance of place or lapse of time can lessen the friendship of those who are thoroughly persuaded of each other's worth.

— Robert Southey

Only in the agony of parting do we look into the depths of love.

— George Eliot

The best things said come last. People will talk for hours saying nothing much and then linger at the door with words that come with a rush from the heart.

— Alan Alda

Why can't we get all the people together in the world that we really like and then just stay together? I guess that wouldn't work. Someone would leave. Someone always leaves. Then we would have to say good-bye. I hate good-byes. I know what I need. I need more hellos.

— Charles M. Schulz

You and I will meet again,
When we're least expecting it,
One day in some far off place,
I will recognize your face,
I won't say goodbye my friend,
For you and I will meet again.

— Tom Petty

46

Father Quotes

Fatherhood is probably one of the most challenging and rewarding role. Here is a series of wonderful father quotes to show appreciation to the man who's the father to you or your kids. Use these dad quotes in your Father's Day cards, letters and journals.

A father is always making his baby into a little woman. And when she is a woman he turns her back again.

— Enid Bagnold

A man knows when he is growing old because he begins to look like his father.

— Gabriel Garcia Marquez

A man never stands as tall as when he kneels to help a child.

— Knights of Pythagoras

All fathers are invisible in daytime; daytime is ruled by mothers and fathers come out at night.

— Margaret Atwood

Blessed indeed is the man who hears many gentle voices call him father!

— Lydia M. Child

But what is happiness except the simple harmony between a man and the life he leads.

— Albert Camus

Dads are stone skimmers, mud wallowers, water wallopers, ceiling swoopers, shoulder gallopers, upsy-downsy, over-and-through, round-and-about whoosers. Dads are smugglers and secret sharers.

— ***Helen Thomson***

Dads don't need to be tall and broad-shouldered and clever. Love makes them so.

— ***Pam Brown***

Doubly rich is the man still boyish enough to play, laugh and sing as he carries and emanates sunshine along a friendly road.

— ***Charles R. Wiers***

His heritage to his children wasn't words or possessions, but an unspoken treasure, the treasure of his example as a man and a father.

— ***Will Rogers Jr.***

He didn't tell me how to live; he lived, and let me watch him do it.

— ***Clarence Budington Kelland***

It is a wise father that knows his own child.

— ***William Shakespeare***

It is admirable for a man to take his son fishing, but there is a special place in heaven for the father who takes his daughter shopping.

— ***John Sinor***

It is easier for a father to have children than for children to have a real father.

— ***Pope John XXIII***

It is much easier to become a father than to be one.

— ***Kent Nerburn***

It's only when you grow up and step back from him— or leave him for your own home-it's only then that you can measure his greatness and fully appreciate it.

— ***Margaret Truman***

Life doesn't come with an instruction book; that's why we have fathers.

— H. Jackson Brown, Jr.

Men learn while they teach.

— Seneca

My father didn't tell me how to live; he lived, and let me watch him do it.

— Clarence Buddinton Kelland

My father used to play with my brother and me in the yard. Mother would come out and say, "You're tearing up the grass." "We're not raising grass," Dad would reply. "We're raising boys."

— Harmon Killebrew

Old as she was, she still missed her daddy sometimes.

— Gloria Naylor

Of course my father was a great influence on me. He taught me how to read.

— Michael Foot

Of course there were areas of safety; nothing could get at me if I curled up on my father's lap, holding his ear with one thumb tucked into it... All about him was safe.

— Naomi Mitchison

One father is more than a hundred Schoolmasters.

— George Herbert

Sometimes the poorest man leaves his children the richest inheritance.

— Ruth E. Renkel

The father who would taste the essence of his fatherhood must turn back from the plane of his experience, take with him the fruits of his journey and begin again beside his child, marching step by step over the same old road.

— Angelo Patri

The great man is he who does not lose his child's heart.

— Mencius

The lucky man has a daughter as his first child.

— Spanish Proverb

The most important thing that a father can do for his children is to love their mother.

— Theodore M. Hesburgh

There's something like a line of gold thread running through a man's words when he talks to his daughter, and gradually over the years it gets to be long enough for you to pick up in your hands and weave into a cloth that feels like love itself.

— John Gregory Brown

To her the name of father was another name for love.

— Fanny Fern

Up on his shoulders... is where I love to be.

— Michael Carr

What do I owe my father? Everything.

— Henry Van Dyke

When a father gives to his son, both laugh; when a son gives to his father, both cry.

— Jewish Proverb

When I was a boy of fourteen, my father was so ignorant I could hardly stand to have the old man around. But when I got to be twenty-one, I was astonished at how much he had learned in seven years.

— Mark Twain

You know, fathers just have a way of putting everything together.

— Erika Cosby

4 years: My Daddy can do anything!

7 years: My Dad knows a lot...a whole lot.

8 years: My father does not know quite everything.

12 years: Oh well, naturally Father does not know that either.

14 years: Oh, Father? He is hopelessly old-fashioned.

21 years: Oh, that man-he is out of date!

25 years: He knows a little bit about it, but not much.

30 years: I must find out what Dad thinks about it.

35 years: Before we decide, we will get Dad's idea first.

50 years: What would Dad have thought about that?

60 years: My Dad knew literally everything!

65 years: I wish I could talk it over with Dad once more.

— ***Anonymous***

47

Freedom Quotes

Every human has four endowments—self-awareness, conscience, independent will and creative imagination. These give us the ultimate human freedom—the power to choose, to respond, to change. Read through this collection of freedom quotes and find out more about the meaning of true freedom. May you find courage, strength and determination from these freedom quotes, and see that freedom is something to be desired and cherished.

Everything can be taken from a man but one thing; the last of the human freedoms—to choose one's attitude in any given set of circumstances, to choose one's own way.

— ***Viktor Frankl***

Freedom has its life in the hearts, the actions, the spirit of men and so it must be daily earned and refreshed—else like a flower cut from its life-giving roots, it will wither and die.

— ***Dwight D. Eisenhower***

Freedom is always and exclusively freedom for the one who thinks differently.

— ***Rosa Luxemburg***

Freedom is never free.

— ***Author Unknown***

Freedom is not worth having if it does not connote freedom to err.

— ***Mahatma Gandhi***

Freedom is that instant between when someone tells you to do something and when you decide how to respond.

— Jeffrey Borenstein

Freedom is the oxygen of the soul.

— Moshe Dayan

Freedom lies in being bold.

— Robert Frost

History does not teach fatalism. There are moments when the will of a handful of free men breaks through determinism and opens up new roads.

— Charles de Gaulle

In the truest sense, freedom cannot be bestowed; it must be achieved.

— Franklin D. Roosevelt

It is easy to take liberty for granted, when you have never had it taken from you.

— Dick Cheney

Nothing is more difficult, and therefore more precious, than to be able to decide.

— Napoleon Bonaparte

People hardly ever make use of the freedom they have. For example, the freedom of thought. Instead they demand freedom of speech as a compensation.

— Søren Kierkegaard

The fact, in short, is that freedom, to be meaningful in an organised society must consist of an amalgam of hierarchy of freedoms and restraints.

— Samuel Hendel

The secret of happiness is freedom. The secret of freedom is courage.

— Thucydide

There are two freedoms—the false, where a man is free to do what he likes; the true, where he is free to do what he ought.

— Charles Kingsley

You have a choice. Live or die. Every breath is a choice. Every minute is a choice. To be or not to be.

— Chuck Palahniuk

48

Friendship Quotes

Friends, some of the most important people in your life. They are there to cheer you on your victories, to pick you up after shattered pieces, to spur you on after failures and disappointments. You don't need your friends to cure you. You probably need your friends to heal you by opening up their hearts, and warm you with their mere presence. That is friendship. Here is a wonderful series of best friend quotes that will help celebrate the many ups and downs you've shared with your good friends.

A friend can tell you things you don't want to tell yourself.

— *Frances Ward Weller*

A friend is one of the nicest things you can have, and one of the best things you can be.

— *Douglas Pagels*

A friend is one who knows us, but loves us anyway.

— *Fr. Jerome Cummings*

A friend knows the song in my heart and sings it to me when my memory fails.

— *Donna Roberts*

A good friend is a connection to life—a tie to the past, a road to the future, the key to sanity in a totally insane world.

— *Lois Wyse*

A loyal friend laughs at your jokes when they're not so good, and sympathises with your problems when they're not so bad.

— Arnold H. Glasgow

A road to a friend's house is never long.

— Danish proverb

A real friend is someone who walks in when the rest of the world walks out.

— Proverb

A true friend is someone who thinks that you are a good egg even though he knows that you are slightly cracked.

— Bernard Meltzer

A true friend never gets in your way unless you are going down.

— Arnold H. Glasgow

Books, like friends, should be few and well chosen.

— Samuel Paterson

But every road is rough to me that has no friend to cheer it.

— Elizabeth Shane

Certain flaws are necessary for the whole. It would seem strange if old friends lacked certain quirks.

— Goethe

Every gift from a friend is a wish for your happiness.

— Richard Bach

Everybody needs one essential friend.

— Dr. William Glasser

Fate chooses our relatives, we choose our friends.

— Jacques Delille

Friends can be said to "fall in like" with as profound a thud as romantic partners fall in love.

— Letty Cottin Pogrebin

Friendships are fragile things, and require as much handling as any other fragile and precious thing.

— Randolph S. Bourne

Friendships begin because, even without words, we understand how someone feels.

— Joan Walsh Anglund

Friendship has no name but love.

— Habib Sahabib

Friendship makes prosperity more brilliant, and lightens adversity by dividing and sharing it.

— Cicero

Good company, lively conversation, and the endearments of friendship fill the mind with great pleasure.

— Edmund Burke

If you'd be beloved, make yourself amiable. A true friend is the best possession.

— Benjamin Franklin

In a true friend you find a second self.

— Isabelle Norton

In everyone's life, at some time, our inner fire goes out. It is then burst into flame by an encounter with another human being. We should all be thankful for those people who rekindle the inner spirit.

— Schweitzer

In the hour of misery, the eye turns to friendship. In the hour of gladness, what is our want? It is friendship.

— Walter S. Landor

In the sweetness of friendship let there be laughter, for in the dew of little things the heart finds its morning and is refreshed.

— Kahlil Gibran

It is one of the blessings of old friends that you can afford to be stupid with them.

— Ralph Waldo Emerson

Laughter is the shortest distance between two friends.

— Victor Borge

Like creativity, friendship is a sudden spark, appreciated and protected. Chance provides the opportunity; care preserves the light.

— Timothy White

My friends are my estate.

— Emily Dickinson

Never shall I forget the days I spent with you. Continue to be my friend, as you will always find me yours.

— Ludwig Van Beethoven

Of all things which wisdom provides to make life entirely happy, the greatest is the possession of friendship.

— Epicurus

Only friends will tell you the truths you need to hear to make your life bearable.

— Francine Du Plessix Gray

Only your real friends will tell you when your face is dirty.

— Sicilian Proverb

Plant a seed of friendship; reap a bouquet of happiness.

— Lois L. Kaufman

Remember, we all stumble, every one of us. That's why it's a comfort to go hand in hand.

— Emily Kimbrough

Remember, the greatest gift is not found in a store nor under a tree, but in the hearts of true friends.

— Cindy Lew

Shared joy is a double joy; shared sorrow is half a sorrow.

— Swedish Proverb

"Stay" is a charming word in a friend's vocabulary.

— Louisa May Alcott

Silences make the real conversations between friends. Not the saying but the never needing to say is what counts.

— Margaret Lee Runbeck

Sometimes being a friend means mastering the art of timing. There is a time for silence. A time to let go and allow people to hurl themselves into their own destiny. And a time to prepare to pick up the pieces when it's all over.

— Octavia Butler

That friend, given to you by circumstances over which you have not control, was God's own gift.

— Fredrick Robertson

The friend who holds your hand and says the wrong thing is made of dearer stuff than the one who stays away.

— Barbara Kingsolver

The mere chink of cups and saucers turns the mind to happy repose.

— George Gissie

The most beautiful discovery that true friends can make is that they can grow separately without growing apart.

— Elizabeth Foley

The most called-upon prerequisite of a friend is an accessible ear.

— Maya Angelou

The truth is friendship is every bit as sacred and eternal as marriage.

— Katherine Mansfield

There is no trouble so great or grave that cannot be much diminished by a nice cup of tea.

— Bernard-Paul Heroux

To know someone here or there with whom you can feel there is understanding in spite of distances or thoughts unexpressed—that can make this life a garden.

— Goethe

To listen closely and reply well is the highest perfection we are able to attain in the art of conversation.

— François, duc de La Rochefoucauld

True friendship comes when silence between two people is comfortable.

— Dave Tyson Gentry

We are all travellers in the wilderness of this world, and the best that we can find in our travels is an honest friend.

— Robert Louis Stevenson

Who finds a faithful friend, finds a treasure.

— Jewish Saying

Wishing to be friends is quick work, but friendship is a slow ripening fruit.

— Aristotle

Without wearing any mask we are conscious of, we have a special face for each friend.

— Oliver Wendell Holmes

You can always tell a real friend; when you've made a fool of yourself he doesn't feel you've done a permanent job.

— Laurence J. Peter

You can make more friends in two months by becoming interested in other people than you can by trying to get other people interested in you.

— Dale Carnegie

You make me proud to spell my name woman... you make me proud to be your friend...

— Oprah Winfrey

Your friendship is better than chocolate! Well, anyway, it's right up there.

— Julie Sutton

49

Funny Quotes

As you try your best to juggle with work, kids, family, housework, friends, hobbies and a zillion of other stuff, let some of these funny quotations and sometimes silly quotes relax you and bring some light-heartedness into your day. Here is a collection of funny quotes and funny thoughts to tickle your funny bone.

A bank is a place where they lend you an umbrella in fair weather and ask for it back when it begins to rain.

— ***Robert Frost***

A woman is like a tea bag—you never know how strong she is until she gets in hot water.

— ***Eleanor Roosevelt***

Advice is what we ask for when we already know the answer but wish we didn't.

— ***Erica Jong***

An eye for an eye makes the whole world blind.

— ***Mahatma Gandhi***

A fanatic is one who can't change his mind and won't change the subject.

— ***Winston Churchill***

Always and never are two words you should always remember never to use.

— ***Wendell Johnson***

Always forgive your enemies—nothing annoys them so much.

— ***Oscar Wilde***

Always remember that you are absolutely unique. Just like everyone else.

— ***Margaret Mead***

Beauty isn't worth thinking about; what's important is your mind. You don't want a fifty-dollar haircut on a fifty-cent head.

— ***Garrison Keillor***

Buy land. They've stopped making it.

— ***Mark Twain***

By the time you're eighty years old you've learned everything. You only have to remember it.

— ***George Burns***

By working faithfully eight hours a day, you may get to be a boss and work twelve hours a day.

— ***Robert Frost***

Clothes make the man. Naked people have little or no influence on society.

— ***Mark Twain***

Consider the postage stamp, my son. It secures success through its ability to stick to one thing till it gets there.

— ***Josh Billings***

Everyone told me to pass on Speed because it was a 'bus movie'.

— ***Sandra Bullock***

Experience is the name everyone gives to their mistakes.

— ***Oscar Wilde***

Experts say you should never hit your children in anger. When is a good time? When you're feeling festive?

— ***Roseanne Barr***

For some strange reason, no matter where I go, the place is always called "here".

— ***Ashleigh Brilliant***

Having a baby changes the way you view your in-laws. I love it when they come to visit now. They can hold the baby and I can go out.

— ***Matthew Broderick***

He who laughs, lasts.

— ***Mary Pettibone Poole***

If you cannot get rid of the family skeleton, you may as well make it dance.

— ***George Bernard Shaw***

If you want something said, ask a man; if you want something done, ask a woman.

— ***Margaret Thatcher***

If you rest, you rust.

— ***Helen Hayes***

I'm an excellent housekeeper. Every time I get a divorce, I keep the house.

— ***Zsa Zsa Gabor***

It's better to live one day as a lion, than a hundred as a sheep.

— ***Benito Mussollini***

I've been on a calendar, but I've never been on time.

— ***Marilyn Munroe***

My life has been filled with terrible misfortune; most of which never happened.

— ***Montaigne***

My theory is that if you look confident you can pull off anything—even if you have no clue what you're doing.

— ***Jessica Alba***

Never go to a doctor whose office plants have died.

— ***Erma Bombeck***

Of all the things I've lost, I miss my mind the most.

— Mark Twain

One of the keys to happiness is a bad memory.

— Rita Mae Brown

Some cause happiness wherever they go; others, whenever they go.

— Oscar Wilde

Some people never go crazy. What truly horrible lives they must lead.

— Charles Bukowski

The ability to quote is a serviceable substitute for wit.

— Somerset Maugham

The advantage of a bad memory is that one enjoys several times the same good things for the first time.

— Friedrich Nietzsche

The elevator to success is out of order. You'll have to use the stairs... one step at a time.

— Joe Girard

The difference between perseverance and obstinacy is that one often comes from a strong will, and the other from a strong won't.

— Henry Ward Beecher

The first law of dietetics seems to be: if it tastes good, it's bad for you.

— Issac Asimov

The hardest years in life are those between ten and seventy.

— Helen Hayes (at 73)

The main thing is keeping the main thing the main thing.

— German Proverb

The nicest thing about quotes is that they give us a nodding acquaintance with the originator which is often socially impressive.

— Kenneth Williams

Those who dance are considered insane by those who cannot hear the music.

— George Carlin

To be happy with a man you must understand him a lot and love him a little. To be happy with a woman you must love her a lot and not try to understand her at all.

— Helen Rowland

To solve the human equation, we need to add love, subtract hate, multiply good, and divide between truth and error.

— Janet Coleman

Until I was 13, I thought my name was 'Shut Up.'

— Joe Namath

When I was young I was called a rugged individualist. When I was in my fifties I was considered eccentric. Here I am doing and saying the same things I did then and I'm labelled senile.

— George Burns

We don't stop playing because we grow old; We grow old because we stop playing.

— George Bernard Shaw

We spend the first twelve months of our children's lives teaching them to walk and talk and the next twelve telling them to sit down and shut up.

— Phyllis Diller

When everyone thinks alike, no one thinks very much.

— Walter Lippmann

When in doubt, make a fool of yourself. There is a microscopically thin line between being brilliantly creative and acting like the most gigantic idiot on earth. So, what the hell, leap!

— Cynthia Heimel

When women are depressed they either eat or go shopping. Men invade another country.

— Elayne Boosler

Whether women are better than men I cannot say—but I can say they are certainly no worse.

— Golda Meir

Why get married and make one man miserable when I can stay single and make thousands miserable?

— Carrie Snow

Wise men talk because they have something to say. Fools talk because they have to say something.

— Plato

Woman are meant to be loved, not to be understood.

— Oscar Wilde

Women complain about premenstrual syndrome, but I think of it as the only time of the month that I can be myself.

— Roseanne Barr

Women dress alike all over the world: they dress to be annoying to other women.

— Elsa Schiaparelli

50

Get Well Quotes

In times of sickness, it is easy to get stuck on words. Let the healing quotes listed below give you some idea of what to write about in your cards and well wishes. Some will fit nicely into your cards, some will work better as encouraging thoughts.

An early morning walk is a blessing for the whole day.

— Henry David Thoreau

Be careful when reading health books; you may die of a misprint.

— Mark Twain

Get well cards have become so humorous that if you don't get sick you're missing half the fun.

— Flip Wilson

I enjoy convalescence. It is the part that makes the illness worth while.

— George Bernard Shaw

I reckon being ill as one of the great pleasures of life, provided one is not too ill and is not obliged to work till one is better.

— Samuel Butler

I wonder why you can always read a doctor's bill and you can never read his prescription.

— Finley Peter Dunne

Pain is inevitable. Suffering is optional.

— ***M. Kathleen Casey***

Sleep, riches, and health to be truly enjoyed must be interrupted.

— ***Johann Paul Friedrich Richter***

The art of medicine consists of amusing the patient while nature cures the disease.

— ***Voltaire***

The best of healers is good cheer.

— ***Pindus***

The greatest healing therapy is friendship and love.

— ***Hubert Humphrey***

The power of love to change bodies is legendary, built into folklore, common sense, and everyday experience. Love moves the flesh, it pushes matter around.... Throughout history, "tender loving care" has uniformly been recognised as a valuable element in healing.

— ***Larry Dossey***

The treatment is really a cooperative of a trinity—the patient, the doctor and the inner doctor.

— ***Ralph Bircher***

There is no medicine like hope, no incentive so great, and no tonic so powerful as expectation of something tomorrow.

— ***Orison Swett Marden***

Time is the best doctor.

— ***Yiddish Proverb***

Warning: Humor may be hazardous to your illness.

— ***Ellie Katz***

You have a cough? Go home tonight, eat a whole box of Ex-Lax—tomorrow you'll be afraid to cough.

— ***Pearl Williams***

Your never know how much they care until you are under the weather.

— ***C. Kohler***

51

Giving Quotes

Many people cling to things. Yet there is many who lovingly share what they have. There is many occasions where you have to give it away. To your kids, your friends, your family, your work and so on. Here is a wonderful collection of giving quotes that will speak of the essence of giving it away and yet receiving a lot in return.

Be generous with kindly words, especially about those who are absent.

*— **Johann Wolfgang von Goethe***

Blessed are those who can give without remembering and take without forgetting.

*— **Elizabeth Asquith Bibesco***

Generosity consists not the sum given, but the manner in which it is bestowed.

*— **Author Unknown***

Give what you have. To someone, it may be better than you dare to think.

*— **Henry Wadsworth Longfellow***

I have found that among its other benefits, giving liberates the soul of the giver.

*— **Maya Angelou***

In helping others, we shall help ourselves, for whatever good we give out completes the circle and comes back to us.

— Flora Edwards

It's not how much we give but how much love we put into giving.

— Mother Teresa

One of the sanest, surest, and most generous joys of life comes from being happy over the good fortune of others.

— Robert A. Heinlein

Real generosity is doing something nice for someone who will never find out.

— Frank A. Clark

Real generosity toward the future lies in giving all to the present.

— Albert Camus

To know when to be generous and when to be firm— this is wisdom.

— Elbert Hubbard

To the generous mind the heaviest debt is that of gratitude, when it is not in our power to repay it.

— Benjamin Franklin

The service we render to others is really the rent we pay for our room on this earth. It is obvious that man is himself a traveler; that the purpose of this world is not 'to have and to hold' but 'to give and serve."

— Sir Wilfred T. Grinfell

The value of a man resides in what he gives and not in what he is capable of receiving.

— Albert Einstein

The wise man does not lay up his own treasures. The more he gives to others, the more he has for his own.

— Lao Tzu

There is overwhelming evidence that the higher the level of self-esteem, the more likely one will be to treat others with respect, kindness, and generosity.

— Nathaniel Branden

There is a wonderful mythical law of nature that the three things we crave most in life — happiness, freedom, and peace of mind — are always attained by giving them to someone else.

— Peyton Conway March

We make a living by what we get, but we make a life by what we give.

— Winston Churchill

Whatever you spend is gone. What you keep, someone else gets. What you give is yours forever.

— Dr. Wil Rose

You give but little when you give of your possessions. It is when you give of yourself that you truly give.

— Kahlil Gibran

52

Grandmother Quotes

Kids adore their grandmas and grandpas with a passion. And they have a good reason for loving so. Simply because grandparents return the favour with great devotion and loads of affection. Grandparents bring about a side that you probably wish that's how your parents dealt with you while you were a child. Abundance of indulgence and unwavering love. Express your feelings for your grandparents or help bridge the generations between your parents and your kids with grandparent quotes.

A child needs a grandparent, anybody's grandparent, to grow a little more securely into an unfamiliar world.

— *Charles and Ann Morse*

A grandma's name is little less in love than is the doting title of a mother.

— *William Shakespeare*

A Grandmother is a safe haven.

— *Suzette Haden Elgin*

A grandmother pretends she doesn't know who you are on Halloween.

— *Erma Bombeck*

A house needs a grandma in it.

— *Louisa May Alcott*

An hour with your grandchildren can make you feel young again. Anything longer than that, and you start to age quickly.

— *Gene Perret*

Becoming a grandmother is wonderful. One moment you're just a mother. The next you are all-wise and prehistoric.

— *Pam Brown*

Being pretty on the inside means you don't hit your brother and you eat all your peas—that's what my grandma taught me.

— *Lord Chesterfield*

By the time the youngest children have learned to keep the house tidy, the oldest grandchildren are on hand to tear it to pieces.

— *Christopher Morley*

Few things are more delightful than grandchildren fighting over your lap.

— *Doug Larson*

Grandchildren are God's way of compensating us for growing old.

— *Mary H. Waldrip*

Grandchildren are the dots that connect the lines from generation to generation.

— *Lois Wyse*

Grandchildren don't stay young forever, which is good because Pop-pops have only so many horsey rides in them.

— *Gene Perret*

Grandma always made you feel she had been waiting to see just you all day and now the day was complete.

— *Marcy DeMaree*

Grandparents are there to help the child get into mischief they haven't thought of yet.

— *Gene Perret*

I loved their home. Everything smelled older, worn but safe; the food aroma had baked itself into the furniture.

— *Susan Strasberg*

If becoming a grandmother was only a matter of choice, I should advise every one of you straight away to become one. There is no fun for old people like it!

— *Hannah Whithall Smith*

If nothing is going well, call your grandmother.

— *Italian Proverb*

If your baby is "beautiful and perfect, never cries or fusses, sleeps on schedule and burps on demand, an angel all the time," you're the grandma.

— *Teresa Bloomingdale*

It is as grandmothers that our mothers come into the fullness of their grace.

— *Christopher Morley*

Just about the time a woman thinks her work is done, she becomes a grandmother.

— *Edward H. Dreschnack*

My grandchild has taught me what true love means. It means watching Scooby-Doo cartoons while the basketball game is on another channel.

— *Gene Perret*

My grandfather was a wonderful role model. Through him I got to know the gentle side of men.

— *Sarah Long*

Nobody can do for little children what grandparents do. Grandparents sort of sprinkle stardust over the lives of little children.

— *Alex Haley*

One of the most powerful handclasps is that of a new grandbaby around the finger of a grandfather.

— *Joy Hargrove*

Surely, two of the most satisfying experiences in life must be those of being a grandchild or a grandparent.

— *Donald A. Norberg*

The idea that no one is perfect is a view most commonly held by people with no grandchildren.

— ***Doug Larson***

The reason grandchildren and grandparents get along so well is that they have a common enemy.

— ***Sam Levenson***

They say genes skip generations. Maybe that's why grandparents find their grandchildren so likeable.

— ***Joan McIntosh***

To show a child what has once delighted you, to find the child's delight added to your own, so that there is now a double delight seen in the glow of trust and affection, this is happiness.

— ***J.B. Priestley***

Uncles and aunts, and cousins, are all very well, and fathers and mothers are not to be despised; but a grandmother, at holiday time, is worth them all.

— ***Fanny Fern***

We should all have one person who knows how to bless us despite the evidence, Grandmother was that person to me.

— ***Phyllis Theroux***

What a bargain grandchildren are! I give them my loose change, and they give me a million dollars' worth of pleasure.

— ***Gene Perret***

What children need most are the essentials that grandparents provide in abundance. They give unconditional love, kindness, patience, humor, comfort, lessons in life. And, most importantly, cookies.

— ***Rudolph Giuliani***

When a child is born, so are grandmothers.

— ***Judith Levy***

When grandparents enter the door, discipline flies out the window.

— ***Ogden Nash***

53

Habit Quotes

Many of us might go about our daily lives without paying attention to our lifetime of habits. Habits once formed, tend to stick around for a long time. Habits are easy to fall back on, because we don't need to think. Habits can make or break our success, depending on their nature. This collection will encourage us to be more mindful of our habits as they have the power to shape our character.

A habit is something you can do without thinking—which is why most of us have so many of them.

— Frank A. Clark

A nail is driven out by another nail; habit is overcome by habit.

— Latin Proverb

Character is long-standing habit.

— Plutarch

Cultivate only the habits that you are willing should master you.

— Elbert Hubbard

Excellence is not a singular act, but a habit. You are what you repeatedly do.

— Shaquille O'Neal

First we make our habits, then our habits make us.

— ***Charles C. Noble***

Good habits, once established are just as hard to break as are bad habits.

— ***Robert Puller***

Habit is habit, and not to be flung out of the window by any man, but coaxed downstairs a step at a time.

— ***Mark Twain***

Habit is either the best of servants or the worst of masters.

— ***Nathaniel Emmons***

Habit is stronger than reason.

— ***George Santayana***

I am in the habit of looking not so much to the nature of a gift as to the spirit in which it is offered.

— ***Robert Louis Stevenson***

Motivation is what gets you started. Habit is what keeps you going.

— ***Jim Rohn***

Nothing is stronger than habit.

— ***Ovid***

Our character is basically a composite of our habits. Because they are consistent, often unconscious patterns, they constantly, daily, express our character.

— ***Stephen Covey***

Quality is not an act, it is a habit.

— ***Aristotle***

We are what we repeatedly do. Excellence, then, is not an act, but a habit.

— ***Aristotle***

54

Healing Quotes

Sometimes we hurt. Sometimes our hearts ache. Sometimes we cry out in pain. In your quest to heal and recover from the hurts that are part of life, you may be seeking for words of inspiration to guide you in times of sorrow. Reasons might not make sense during periods of intense pain and suffering, and yet when given time and compassion, the sorrow would somehow lessen in intensity. Getting in touch with nature during times of hurt is very soothing for the soul. This collection of healing quotes will bring a dose of comfort to your soul.

> A lot of people say they want to get out of pain, and I'm sure that's true, but they aren't willing to make healing a high priority. They aren't willing to look inside to see the source of their pain in order to deal with it.
>
> — ***Lindsay Wagner***

> All healing is first a healing of the heart.
>
> — ***Carl Townsend***

> Although the world is full of suffering, it is also full of the overcoming of it.
>
> — ***Helen Keller***

> Eventually you will come to understand that love heals everything, and love is all there is.
>
> — ***Gary Zukav***

For your born writer, nothing is so healing as the realisation that he has come upon the right word.

— Catherine Drinker Bowen

Forgiving does not erase the bitter past. A healed memory is not a deleted memory. Instead, forgiving what we cannot forget creates a new way to remember. We change the memory of our past into a hope for our future.

— Lewis B. Smedes

Healing is a matter of time, but it is sometimes also a matter of opportunity.

— Hippocrates

Healing may not be so much about getting better, as about letting go of everything that isn't you—all of the expectations, all of the beliefs—and becoming who you are.

— Rachel Naomi Remen

"Healing," Papa would tell me, "is not a science, but the intuitive art of wooing nature."

— W.H. Auden

Healing takes courage, and we all have courage, even if we have to dig a little to find it.

— Tori Amos

Healing yourself is connected with healing others.

— Yoko Ono

Humour is healing.

— Brad Garrett

I am not bound for any public place, but for ground of my own where I have planted vines and orchard trees, and in the heat of the day climbed up into the healing shadow of the woods.

— Wendell Berry

I had no idea that mothering my own child would be so healing to my own sadness from my childhood.

— Susie Bright

I have a couple of girlfriends who are like, healing. We take care of each other. They know when I need to be taken care of.

— *Maggie Gyllenhaal*

I think music in itself is healing. It's an explosive expression of humanity. It's something we are all touched by. No matter what culture we're from, everyone loves music.

— *Billy Joel*

I've experienced several different healing methodologies over the years—counseling, self-help seminars, and I've read a lot—but none of them will work unless you really want to heal.

— *Lindsay Wagner*

Live your life from your heart. Share from your heart. And your story will touch and heal people's souls.

— *Melody Beattie*

Love one another and help others to rise to the higher levels, simply by pouring out love. Love is infectious and the greatest healing energy.

— *Sai Baba*

Music is very important. It's important as a tool for learning, it can be a tool for healing, it can be no telling what, as long as we remain free to be able to create the music, to be able to experiment and to really research, and to really get time to develop the music.

— *Lester Bowie*

Our sorrows and wounds are healed only when we touch them with compassion.

— *Buddha*

The art of healing comes from nature, not from the physician. Therefore the physician must start from nature, with an open mind.

— *Philipus Aureolus Paracelsus*

The greatest healing therapy is friendship and love.

— *Hubert H. Humphrey*

The practice of forgiveness is our most important contribution to the healing of the world.

— *Marianne Williamson*

The soul is healed by being with children.

— *Fyodor Dostoyevsky*

The words of kindness are more healing to a drooping heart than balm or honey.

— *Sarah Fielding*

There is something beautiful about all scars of whatever nature. A scar means the hurt is over, the wound is closed and healed, done with.

— *Harry Crews*

To heal from the inside out is the key.

— *Wynonna Judd*

We need to give each other the space to grow, to be ourselves, to exercise our diversity. We need to give each other space so that we may both give and receive such beautiful things as ideas, openness, dignity, joy, healing, and inclusion.

— *Max de Pree*

55

Heart Quotes

Here is a collection of wonderful quotes about the wisdom of your heart and the importance of listening to one's heart. If you are one who wants to follow your heart but are fearful of the risks you'll be taking, this series of heart quotes will shed some light on the wisdom of your heart.

A flower without a stem, is beauty waiting to die. A heart without love, is a tear waiting to cry.

— *Octavio Paz*

A good heart is better than all the heads in the world.

— *Edward George Earle Bulwer-Lytton*

A joyful heart is the inevitable result of a heart burning with love.

— *Mother Teresa*

A kind heart is a fountain of gladness making everything in its vicinity freshen into smiles.

— *Washington Irving*

A person's world is only as big as their heart.

— *Tanya A. Moore*

All paths lead nowhere, so it is important to choose a path that has heart.

— *Carlos Castaneda*

And you would accept the seasons of your heart just as you have always accepted that seasons pass over your fields and you would watch with serenity through the winters of your grief.

— ***Kahlil Gibran***

Beware what you set your heart upon, for it surely shall be yours.

— ***Ralph Waldo Emerson***

Each one sees what he carries in his heart.

— ***Johann Wolfgang von Goethe***

Educating the mind without educating the heart is no education at all.

— ***Aristotle***

Everyone has been made for some particular work, and the desire for that work has been put in every heart.

— ***Mevlana Rumi***

Find the seed at the bottom of your heart and bring forth a flower.

— ***Shigenori Kameoka***

Go to your bosom: Knock there, and ask your heart what it doth know.

— ***William Shakespeare***

He who cherishes a beautiful vision, a lofty ideal in his heart, will one day realise it.

— ***James Allen***

I would rather have eyes that cannot see; ears that cannot hear; lips that cannot speak, than a heart that cannot love.

— ***Robert Tizon***

If I create from the heart, nearly everything works; if from the head, almost nothing.

— ***Marc Chagall***

If wrinkles must be written upon our brow, let them not be written upon the heart; the spirit should not grow old.

— ***James A. Garfield***

If your head tells you one thing, and your heart tells you another, before you do anything, you should first decide whether you have a better head or a better heart.

— ***Marilyn vos Savant***

In a full heart there is room for everything, and in an empty heart there is room for nothing.

— ***Antonio Porchia***

In prayer it is better to have a heart without words than words without a heart.

— ***Mahatma Gandhi***

It is only with the heart that one can see rightly; what is essential is invisible to the eye.

— ***Antoine de Saint-Exupery***

Nobody has ever measured, not even poets, how much the heart can hold.

— ***Zelda Fitzgerald***

One of the hardest things in life is having words in your heart that you can't utter.

— ***James Earl Jones***

Only do what your heart tells you.

— ***Princess Diana***

Tell your heart that the fear of suffering is worse than the suffering itself. And no heart has ever suffered when it goes in search of its dream.

— ***Paulo Coelho***

The best and most beautiful things in the world cannot be seen or even touched. They must be felt with the heart.

— ***Helen Keller***

The heart has reasons that reason does not understand.

— ***Jacques Benigne Bossuel***

The heart is forever making the head its fool.

— ***François de la Rochefoucauld***

The human heart feels things the eyes cannot see, and knows what the mind cannot understand.

— Robert Valett

The less you open your heart to others, the more your heart suffers.

— Deepak Chopra

There are many things in life that will catch your eye, but only a few will catch your heart...pursue those.

— Michael Nolan

What is uttered from the heart alone,

Will win the hearts of others to your own.

— Johann Wolfgang von Goethe

What your heart thinks is great, is great. The soul's emphasis is always right.

— Ralph Waldo Emerson

When you stop putting yourself on the line, and you don't touch your own heart, how do you expect to touch other people?

— Tori Amos

Wherever you go, go with all your heart.

— Confucius

56

Holiday Quotes

Holidays give a good, legitimate reason to celebrate with family and friends. The holiday quotes given below will remind you that holidays are seasonal breaks that fill you up with anticipation.

> Are you willing to believe that love is the strongest thing in the world—stronger than hate, stronger than evil, stronger than death—and that the blessed life which began in Bethlehem nineteen hundred years ago is the image and brightness of the Eternal Love? Then you can keep Christmas.
>
> — ***Henry Van Dyke***

> As we struggle with shopping lists and invitations, compounded by December's bad weather, it is good to be reminded that there are people in our lives who are worth this aggravation, and people to whom we are worth the same.
>
> — ***Donald E. Westlake***

> At Christmas play and make good cheer, for Christmas comes but once a year.
>
> — ***Thomas Tusser***

> Blessed is the season which engages the whole world in a conspiracy of love.
>
> — ***Hamilton Wright Mabie***

Christmas gift suggestions: To your enemy, forgiveness. To an opponent, tolerance. To a friend, your heart. To a customer, service. To all, charity. To every child, a good example. To yourself, respect.

— ***Oren Arnold***

Christmas is for children. But it is for grownups too. Even if it is a headache, a chore, and nightmare, it is a period of necessary defrosting of chill and hide-bound hearts.

— ***Lenora Mattingly Weber***

Christmas is not a time nor a season, but a state of mind. To cherish peace and goodwill, to be plenteous in mercy, is to have the real spirit of Christmas.

— ***Calvin Coolidge***

Every piece of the universe, even the tiniest little snow crystal, matters somehow. I have a place in the pattern, and so do you...Thinking of you this holiday season!

— ***T.A. Barron***

I wish we could put up some of the Christmas spirit in jars and open a jar of it every month.

— ***Harlan Miller***

If I were a medical man, I should prescribe a holiday to any patient who considered his work important.

— ***Bertrand Russell***

Love the giver more than the gift.

— ***Brigham Young***

May your walls know joy, may every room hold laughter, and every window open to great possibility

— ***Mary Anne Radmacher***

Our hearts grow tender with childhood memories and love of kindred, and we are better throughout the year for having, in spirit, become a child again at Christmas-time.

— ***Laura Ingalls Wilder***

The best and most beautiful things in the world cannot be seen or even touched. They must be felt with the heart. Wishing you happiness.

– ***Helen Keller***

The holiest of all holidays are those
Kept by ourselves in silence and apart;
The secret anniversaries of the heart,
When the full river of feeling overflows;—
The happy days unclouded to their close;
The sudden joys that our of darkness start
As flames from ashes; swift desires that dart
Like swallows singing down each wind that blows!

– ***Henry Wadsworth Longfellow***

The joy of brightening other lives, bearing each others' burdens, easing other's loads and supplanting empty hearts and lives with generous gifts becomes for us the magic of Christmas.

– ***W. C. Jones***

There is no ideal Christmas; only the one Christmas you decide to make as a reflection of your values, desires, affections, traditions.

– ***Bill McKibben***

This is my wish for you: peace of mind, prosperity through the year, happiness that multiplies, health for you and yours, fun around every corner, energy to chase your dreams, joy to fill your holidays!

– ***D.M. Dellinger***

Time for work—yet take much holiday for art's and friendship's sake.

– ***George James De Wilde***

To many people holidays are not voyages of discovery, but a ritual of reassurance.

– ***Philip Andrew Adams***

57

Honesty Quotes

Honesty quotes highlight the importance of this quality in maintaining one's authenticity. If someone is being honest to others at all times, then that person will have no worries about forgetting what was mentioned to others. We usually seek for honesty in relationships and it is probably one of the building blocks of a strong relationship. You may find strength with these honesty quotes.

Almost any difficulty will move in the face of honesty. When I am honest I never feel stupid. And when I am honest I am automatically humble.

— ***Hugh Prather***

Be Silly. Be honest. Be kind.

— ***Ralph Waldo Emerson***

Each time you are honest and conduct yourself with honesty, a success force will drive you toward greater success. Each time you lie, even with a little white lie, there are strong forces pushing you toward failure.

— ***Joseph Sugarman***

Freedom is for honest people. No man who is not himself honest can be free – he is his own trap.

— ***L. Ron Hubbard***

Honest disagreement is often a good sign of progress.

— ***Mahatma Gandhi***

Deal honestly and objectively with yourself; intellectual honesty and personal courage are the hallmarks of great character.

– Brian Tracey

Honest hearts produce honest actions.

– Brigham Young

Honesty is the first chapter of the book of wisdom.

– Thomas Jefferson

I am a big believer in the 'mirror test.' All that matters is if you can look in the mirror and honestly tell the person you see there, that you've done your best.

– John McKay

I have found that being honest is the best technique I can use. Right up front, tell people what you're trying to accomplish and what you're willing to sacrifice to accomplish it.

– Lee Iacocca

If you tell the truth you don't have to remember anything.

– Mark Twain

Level with your child by being honest. Nobody spots a phony quicker than a child.

– Mary MacCracken

No one can lie, no one can hide anything, when he looks directly into someone's eyes.

– Paulo Coelho

One of the hardest things in this world is to admit you are wrong. And nothing is more helpful in resolving a situation than its frank admission.

– Benjamin Disraeli

Our lives improve only when we take chances—and the first and most difficult risk we can take is to be honest with ourselves.

– Walter Anderson

People who are brutally honest get more satisfaction out of the brutality than out of the honesty.

— *Richard J. Needham*

Pretty much all the honest truth telling in the world is done by children.

— *Oliver Wendell*

Slander cannot destroy an honest man—when the flood recedes the rock is there.

— *Chinese Proverbs*

The man who cannot endure to have his errors and shortcomings brought to the surface and made known, but tries to hide them, is unfit to walk the highway of truth.

— *James Allen*

The truth needs so little rehearsal.

— *Barbara Kingsolver*

Today I bent the truth to be kind, and I have no regret, for I am far surer of what is kind than I am of what is true.

— *Robert Brault*

Walking your talk is a great way to motivate yourself. No one likes to live a lie. Be honest with yourself, and you will find the motivation to do what you advise others to do.

— *Vince Poscente*

What is uttered from the heart alone, Will win the hearts of others to your own.

— *Johann Wolfgang von Goethe*

When in doubt, tell the truth.

— *Mark Twain*

When something that honest is said it usually needs a few minutes of silence to dissipate.

— *Pamela Ribon*

When you stretch the truth, watch out for the snapback.

— *Bill Copeland*

58

Happiness Quotes

Many people are seeking for happiness and the harder you search for happiness, the more it seems to elude you. You can be happy. Right at this moment. It is your choice. Happiness is not something that we chase after endlessly. It is within you. Get inspired by this collection of happiness quotes that point out the ingredients for a happy life.

A great obstacle to happiness is to expect too much happiness.

— ***Bernard de Fontenelle***

A happy person is not a person in a certain set of circumstances, but rather a person with a certain set of attitudes.

— ***Hugh Downs***

A man is not rightly conditioned until he is a happy, healthy, and prosperous being; and happiness, health, and prosperity are the result of a harmonious adjustment of the inner with the outer of the man with his surroundings.

— ***James Allen***

All seasons are beautiful for the person who carries happiness within.

— ***Horace Friess***

Cheerfulness is what greases the axles of the world. Don't go through life creaking.

— ***H.W. Byles***

Enjoy the little things, for one day you may look back and realise they were the big things.

— ***Robert Brault***

Finding happiness is like finding yourself. You don't find happiness, you make happiness. You choose happiness. Self-actualisation is a process of discovering who you are, who you want to be and paving the way to happiness by doing what brings you the most meaning and contentment to your life over the long run.

— ***David Leonhardt***

Happiness cannot come from without. It must come from within. It is not what we see and touch or that which others do for us which makes us happy; it is that which we think and feel and do, first for the other fellow and then for ourselves.

— ***Helen Keller***

Happiness comes from spiritual wealth, not material wealth... Happiness comes from giving, not getting. If we try hard to bring happiness to others, we cannot stop it from coming to us also. To get joy, we must give it, and to keep joy, we must scatter it.

— ***John Templeton***

Happiness comes when your work and words are of benefit to yourself and others.

— ***Buddha***

Happiness is as a butterfly which, when pursued, is always beyond our grasp, but which if you will sit down quietly, may alight upon you.

— ***Nathaniel Hawthorne***

Happiness is a conscious choice, not an automatic response.

— ***Mildred Barthel***

Happiness is a matter of one's most ordinary and everyday mode of consciousness being busy and lively and unconcerned with self.

— Iris Murdoch

Happiness is not a station you arrive at, but a manner of travelling.

— Margaret Lee Runbeck

Happiness is not having what you want, but wanting what you have.

— Anon

Happiness is not something you postpone for the future; it is something you design for the present.

— Jim Rohn

Happiness is the only good. The time to be happy is now. The place to be happy is here. The way to be happy is to make others so.

— Robert G. Ingersoll

Happiness is when what you think, what you say, and what you do are in harmony.

— Mahatma Gandhi

Happiness lies in the joy of achievement and the thrill of creative effort.

Franklin D. Roosevelt

Happiness resides not in possessions and not in gold, the feeling of happiness dwells in the soul.

— Democritus

Happiness, that grand mistress of the ceremonies in the dance of life, impels us through all its mazes and meanderings, but leads none of us by the same route.

— Charles Caleb Colton

If you ever find happiness by hunting for it, you will find it, as the old woman did her lost spectacles, safe on her own nose all the time.

— Josh Billings

It is not easy to find happiness in ourselves, and it is not possible to find it elsewhere.

— ***Agnes Repplier***

It is only possible to live happily ever after on a day to day basis.

— ***Margaret Bonnano***

It isn't what you have, or who you are, or where you are, or what you are doing that makes you happy or unhappy. It is what you think about.

— ***Dale Carnegie***

It makes no difference where you go, there you are. And it makes no difference what you have, there's always more to want. Until you are happy with who you are, you will never be happy because of what you have.

— ***Zig Ziglar***

Let us be grateful to people who make us happy; they are the charming gardeners who make our souls blossom.

— ***Marcel Proust***

Many people have a wrong idea of what constitutes true happiness. It is not attained through self-gratification, but through fidelity to a worthy purpose.

— ***Helen Keller***

Most people are about as happy as they make up their minds to be.

— ***Abraham Lincoln***

Nobody really cares if you're miserable, so you might as well be happy.

— ***Cynthia Nelms***

Often people attempt to live their lives backwards; they try to have more things, or more money, in order to do more of what they want, so they will be happier. The way it actually works is the reverse. You must first be who you really are, then do what you need to do, in order to have what you want.

— ***Margaret Young***

On the whole, the happiest people seem to be those who have no particular cause for being happy except that they are so.

— William R. Inge

Our happiness depends on the habit of mind we cultivate. So practice happy thinking every day. Cultivate the merry heart, develop the happiness habit, and life will become a continual feast.

— Norman Vincent Peale

People spend a lifetime searching for happiness; looking for peace. They chase idle dreams, addictions, religions, even other people, hoping to fill the emptiness that plagues them. The irony is the only place they ever needed to search was within.

— Ramona L. Anderson

People take different roads seeking fulfillment and happiness. Just because they're not on your road doesn't mean they've gotten lost.

— H. Jackson Browne

Plenty of people miss their share of happiness, not because they never found it, but because they didn't stop to enjoy it.

— William Feather

Success is not the key to happiness. Happiness is the key to success. If you love what you are doing, you will be successful.

— Albert Schweitzer

The art of living does not consist in preserving and clinging to a particular mode of happiness, but in allowing happiness to change its form without being disappointed by the change; happiness, like a child, must be allowed to grow up.

— Charles L. Morgan

The best way for a person to have happy thoughts is to count his blessings and not his cash There is no goal better than this one: to know as you lie on your deathbed that you lived your true life, and you did whatever made you happy.

— Steve Chandler

The best way to cheer yourself up is to try to cheer somebody else up.

— Mark Twain

The foolish man seeks happiness in the distance; the wise grows it under his feet.

— James Openheim

The grand essentials of happiness are: something to do, something to love, and something to hope for.

— Allan K. Chalmers

The greatest part of our happiness depends on our dispositions, not our circumstances.

— Martha Washington

The happiest moments of my life have been the few which I have passed at home in the bosom of my family.

— Thomas Jefferson

The pursuit of happiness is a most ridiculous phrase: if you pursue happiness you'll never find it.

— C.P. Snow

There is only one happiness in life, to love and be loved.

— George Sand

There is no cosmetic for beauty like happiness.

— Lady Blessington

This life is yours. Take the power to choose what you want to do and do it well. Take the power to love what you want in life and love it honestly. Take the power to walk in the forest and be a part of nature. Take the power to control your own life. No one else can do it for you. Take the power to make your life happy.

— Susan Polis Schutz

Those who bring sunshine into the lives of others, cannot keep it from themselves.

— James M. Barrie

We act as though comfort and luxury were the chief requirements in life, when all we need to make us really happy is something to be enthusiastic about.

— *Charles Kingsley*

We tend to forget that happiness doesn't come as a result of getting something we don't have, but rather of recognising and appreciating what we do have.

— *Frederick Keonig*

What we call the secret of happiness is no more a secret than our willingness to choose life.

— *Leo Buscaglia*

When one door of happiness closes, another opens; but often we look so long at the closed door that we do not see the one which has been opened for us.

— *Helen Keller*

When we feel love and kindness toward others, it not only makes others feel loved and cared for, but it helps us also to develop inner happiness and peace.

— *Dalai Lama*

When you're happy for no reason, you're unconditionally happy. It's not that your life always looks perfect—it's just that however it looks, you'll still be happy.

— *Marci Shimoff*

When you're really happy, the birds chirp and the sun shines even on cold dark winter nights—and flowers will bloom on a barren land.

— *Grey Livingston*

You need to learn to be happy by nature, because you'll seldom have the chance to be happy by circumstance.

— *Lavetta Sue Wegman*

59

History Quotes

Here is a collection of history quotes that inspires. Whether you are a history buff, or a student trying to comprehend the usefulness of history in one's life, or a scrapbooker wanting to add some quotes to your layouts, may you find the right quote from this collection.

A lot of guys have had a lot of fun joking about Henry Ford because he admitted one time that he didn't know history. He don't know it, but history will know him. He has made more history than his critics ever read.

— ***Will Rogers***

All history becomes subjective; in other words there is properly no history, only biography.

— ***Ralph Waldo Emerson***

Anybody can make history. Only a great man can write it.

— ***Oscar Wilde***

Anyone who believes you can't change history has never tried to write his memoirs.

— ***David Ben Gurion***

Every true history must force us to remember that the past was once as real as the present and as uncertain as the future.

— ***George Macaulay Trevelyan***

Few will have the greatness to bend history itself; but each of us can work to change a small portion of events, and in the total of all those acts will be written the history of this generation.

— ***Robert F. Kennedy***

History, despite its wrenching pain, cannot be unlived, but if faced with courage, need not be lived again.

— ***Maya Angelou***

History is a guide to navigation in perilous times. History is who we are and why we are the way we are.

— ***David C. McCullough***

History is a kind of introduction to more interesting people than we can possibly meet in our restricted lives; let us not neglect the opportunity.

— ***Dexter Perkins***

History is a vast early warning system.

— ***Norman Cousins***

History is merely a list of surprises. It can only prepare us to be surprised yet again.

— ***Kurt Vonnegut***

History is more or less bunk. It's tradition. We don't want tradition. We want to live in the present and the only history that is worth a tinker's damn is the history we make today.

— ***Henry Ford***

History is the only laboratory we have in which to test the consequences of thought.

— ***Etienne Gilson***

History is written by the victors.

— ***Winston Churchill***

History never looks like history when you are living through it.

— ***John W. Gardner***

History will be kind to me for I intend to write it.

— ***Winston Churchill***

I like the dreams of the future better than the history of the past.

— Thomas Jefferson

I think a secure profession for young people is history teacher, because in the future, there will be so much more of it to teach.

— Bill Muse

Ideas shape the course of history.

— John Maynard Keynes

If history were taught in the form of stories, it would never be forgotten.

— Rudyard Kipling

Just as philosophy is the study of other people's misconceptions, so history is the study of other people's mistakes.

— Phillip Guedala

People always seemed to know half of history, and to get it confused with the other half.

— Jane Haddam

People tend to forget that the word "history" contains the word "story".

— Ken Burns

Remember that all through history the way of truth and love has always won. There have been tyrants and murderers and for a time they seem invincible but in the end, they always fall — think of it, always.

— Mahatma Gandhi

The charm of history and its enigmatic lesson consist in the fact that, from age to age, nothing changes and yet everything is completely different.

— Aldous Huxley

The history of free men is never really written by chance but by choice—their choice.

— Dwight David Eisenhower

Those who cannot learn from history are doomed to repeat it.

— George Santayana

Until lions have their historians, tales of the hunt shall always glorify the hunters.

— African Proverb

We are made wise not by the recollection of our past, but by the responsibility for our future.

— George Bernard Shaw

Well behaved women rarely make history.

— Laurel Thatcher Ulrich

What is history? An echo of the past in the future; a reflex from the future on the past.

— Victor Hugo

Throughout history, it has been the inaction of those who could have acted; the indifference of those who should have known better; the silence of the voice of justice when it mattered most; that has made it possible for evil to triumph.

— Haile Selassie

60

Hope Quotes

Some say that without hope, life will lose its meaning. As Christopher Reeve elegantly puts it across, "Once you choose hope, anything's possible." No matter how tough your days might be, if you still harbour hopes within you, you'll have something precious to hold on to keep you going. Here is a collection of hope quotes that will show that having hopes will brighten up your days and make your dreams seem possible.

"While I breath, I hope".

— ***Latin Proverb***

Expect to have hope rekindled. Expect your prayers to be answered in wondrous ways. The dry seasons in life do not last. The spring rains will come again.

— ***Sarah Ban Breathnach***

He who has health, has hope. And he who has hope, has everything.

— ***Proverb***

He who has never hoped can never despair.

— ***George Bernard Shaw***

Hope begins in the dark, the stubborn hope that if you just show up and try to do the right thing, the dawn will come. You wait and watch and work: you don't give up.

— ***Anne Lamott***

Hope has two beautiful daughters. Their names are anger and courage; anger at the way things are, and courage to see that they do not remain the way they are.

— *Augustine of Hippo*

Hope is a higher heart frequency, and as you begin to re-connect with your heart, hope is waiting to show you new possibilities and arrest the downward spiral of grief and loneliness. Listening to the still small voice in your heart will make hope into a reality.

— *Sara Paddison*

Hope is always available to us. When we feel defeated, we need only take a deep breath and say, "Yes," and hope will reappear.

— *Monroe Forester*

Hope is faith holding out its hand in the dark.

— *George Iles*

Hope is like a road in the country; there was never a road, but when many people walk on it, the road comes into existence.

— *Lin Yutang*

Hope is the dream of a soul awake.

— *French Proverb*

Hope is the most exciting thing in life and if you honestly believe that love is out there, it will come. And even if it doesn't come straight away there is still that chance all through your life that it will.

— *Josh Hartnett*

Hope is the thing with feathers, that perches in the soul, and sings the tune without words, and never stops at all.

— *Emily Dickinson*

Hope never abandons you; you abandon it.

— *George Weinberg*

Hope sees the invisible, feels the intangible and achieves the impossible.

— Anonymous

I find hope in the darkest of days, and focus in the brightest. I do not judge the universe.

— Dalai Lama

If it were not for hopes, the heart would break.

— Thomas Fuller

If you lose hope, somehow you lose the vitality that keeps life moving, you lose that courage to be, that quality that helps you go on in spite of it all. And so today I still have a dream.

— Martin Luther King, Jr

In all things it is better to hope than to despair.

— Johann Wolfgang von Goethe

In three words I can sum up everything I've learned about life. It goes on.

— Robert Frost

Learn from yesterday, live for today, hope for tomorrow.

— Albert Einstein

Listen now to the gentle whispers of hope.

— Charles D. Brodhead

Man can live about forty days without food, about three days without water, about eight minutes without air, but only for one second without hope.

— Author Unknown

No man is beaten until his hope is annihilated, his confidence gone. As long as a man faces life hopefully, confidently, triumphantly, he is not a failure; he is not beaten until he turns his back on life.

— Orison Swett Marden

Practice hope. As hopefulness becomes a habit, you can achieve a permanently happy spirit.

— Norman Vincent Peale

Once you choose hope, anything's possible.

– Christopher Reeve

The Grand essentials of happiness are: something to do, something to love, and something to hope for.

– Allan K. Chalmers

The natural flights of the human mind are not from pleasure to pleasure but from hope to hope.

– Samuel Johnson

The very least you can do in your life is to figure out what you hope for. And the most you can do is live inside that hope.

– Barbara Kingsolve

There is no medicine like hope, no incentive so great, and no tonic so powerful as expectation of something better tomorrow.

– Orison Swett Marden

Those who wish to sing always find a song.

– Proverb

To eat bread without hope is still slowly to starve to death.

– Pearl S. Buck

We are all in the gutter, but some of us are looking at the stars.

– Oscar Wilde

We must accept finite disappointment, but never lose infinite hope.

– Martin Luther King, Jr

What oxygen is to the lungs, such is hope to the meaning of life.

– Emil Brunne

When the heart is enlivened again, it feels like the sun coming out after a week of rainy days. There is hope in the heart that chases the clouds away. Hope is a higher heart frequency and as you begin to reconnect with your heart, hope is waiting to show you new possibilities and arrest the downward spiral of grief and loneliness. It becomes a matter of how soon you want the sun to shine. Listening to the still, small voice in your heart will make hope into a reality.

— ***Sara Paddison***

When the world says, "Give up,"

Hope whispers, "Try it one more time."

— ***Author Unknown***

When you do nothing, you feel overwhelmed and powerless. But when you get involved, you feel the sense of hope and accomplishment that comes from knowing you are working to make things better.

— ***Pauline R. Kezer***

Why shed tears on failures long forgotten when hope looms on the horizon?

— ***Charles Casha***

Your hopes, dreams and aspirations are legitimate. They are trying to take you airborne, above the clouds, above the storms, if you only let them.

— ***William James***

61

Husband Quotes

Are you in love with your husband? Still crazy about your hubby? Here is a collection of inspiring and funny hubby quotes.

A husband is a guy who tells you when you've got on too much lipstick and helps you with your girdle when your hips stick.

— ***Ogden Nash***

A woman who knows how to compose a soup or a salad that is perfectly harmonious in flavour ought to be clever at mixing together the sweet and harsh elements of a man's character, and she will understand how to charm and keep forever her husband's heart and soul.

— ***Berjane***

An archaeologist is the best husband a woman can have. The older she gets the more interested he is in her.

— ***Agatha Christie***

At the end of your life, you will never regret not having passed one more test, not winning one more verdict or not closing one more deal. You will regret time not spent with a husband, a friend, a child, or a parent.

— ***Barbara Bush***

For years my wedding ring has done its job. It has led me not into temptation. It has reminded my husband numerous times at parties that it's time to go home. It has been a source of relief to a dinner companion. It has been a status symbol in the maternity ward.

— Erma Bombeck

He's the funniest, smartest person I know. It doesn't mean he doesn't bug me and I'm sure I bug him sometimes.

— Sarah Jessica Parker

I am happy to know that my husband regards me as a woman and a person.

— Katherine Dunham

I would say that the surest measure of a man's or a woman's maturity is the harmony, style, joy, and dignity he creates in his marriage, and the pleasure and inspiration he provides for his spouse.

— Benjamin McLane Spock

I really take pride in the relationship that I have with my husband.

— Julie Benz

If we must lose wife or husband when we live to our highest right, we lose an unhappy marriage as well, and we gain ourselves. But if a marriage is born between two already self-discovered, what a lovely adventure begins, hurricanes and all.

— Richard Bach

Love is the thing that enables a woman to sing while she mops up the floor after her husband has walked across it in his barn boots.

— Hoosier Farmer

Many marriages would be better if the husband and the wife clearly understood that they are on the same side.

— Zig Ziglar

My husband and I have figured out a really good system about the housework: neither one of us does it.

— Dottie Archibald

My husband says I feed him like he's a god: every meal is a burnt offering.

— Rhonda Hansome

No, I don't understand my husband's theory of relativity, but I know my husband and I know he can be trusted.

— Elsa Einstein

People shop for a bathing suit with more care than they do a husband or wife. The rules are the same. Look for something you'll feel comfortable wearing. Allow for room to grow.

— Erma Bombeck

Smile at each other, smile at your wife, smile at your husband, smile at your children, smile at each other — it doesn't matter who it is — and that will help you to grow up in greater love for each other.

— Mother Teresa

That quiet mutual gaze of a trusting husband and wife is like the first moment of rest or refuge from a great weariness or a great danger—not to be interfered with by speech or action which would distract the sensations from the fresh enjoyment of repose.

— George Eliot

What is a husband? He is the one who, with a touch, can bring back the starlight and glow of years long ago. At least he hopes he can—don't disappoint him.

— Alan Beck

When a man and a woman have an overwhelming passion for each other, it seems to me, in spite of such obstacles dividing them as parents or husband, that they belong to each other in the name of Nature, and are lovers by Divine right, in spite of human convention or the laws.

— Sébastien-Roch Nicolas De Chamfort

When a wife has a good husband it is easily seen in her face.

— Johann Wolfgang von Goethe

62

Indira Gandhi Quotes

Indira Gandhi was the first women Prime Minister of India (from 1966 to 1977 and from 1980 to 1984). Daughter of Jawaharlal Nehru, a hero in winning independence from Britain, Indira Gandhi was also a follower of Gandhi in her early years. Indira Gandhi was elected Prime Minister in 1966, and her administration was often controversial. After using the military to put an end to a Sikh separatist operation, Indira Gandhi was assassinated by her Sikh security guards in 1984. Some of the selected quotes by Indira Gandhi are here.

You must learn to be still in the midst of activity and to be vibrantly alive in repose.

My grandfather once told me that there were two kinds of people: those who do the work and those who take the credit. He told me to try to be in the first group; there was much less competition.

Martyrdom does not end something, it is only a beginning.

You cannot shake hands with a clenched fist.

There are moments in history when brooding tragedy and its dark shadows can be lightened by recalling great moments of the past.

There exists no politician in India daring enough to attempt to explain to the masses that cows can be eaten.

I would say our greatest achievement is to have survived as a free and democratic nation.

I don't mind if my life goes in the service of the nation. If I die today every drop of my blood will invigorate the nation.

To bear many children is considered not only a religious blessing but also an investment. The greater their number, some Indians reason, the more alms they can beg.

The power to question is the basis of all human progress.

Forgiveness is a virtue of the brave.

People tend to forget their duties but remember their rights.

Where there is love there is life.

There is not love where there is no will.

I suppose leadership at one time meant muscles; but today it means getting along with people

Anger is never without an argument, but seldom with a good one.

63

Inspirational Quotes

Have you ever observed nature closely? Have you ever noticed how a seed fights the earth to emerge into a victorious plant? Have you observed how a bird, with precision and hard work, finally manages to build its nest? Nature does not give up. Why should you? If you feel inspired to make a new beginning, read the words of Abraham Lincoln, Voltaire, and Buddha in this collection of inspirational sayings.

Men are born to succeed, not fail.

— Henry David Thoreau

That some achieve great success, is proof to all that others can achieve it as well.

— Abraham Lincoln

The dictionary is the only place where success comes before work.

— Mark Twain

Just don't give up trying to do what you really want to do. Where there is love and inspiration, I don't think you can go wrong.

— Ella Fitzgerald

People rarely succeed unless they have fun in what they are doing.

— Dale Carnegie

A man may conquer a million men in battle but one who conquers himself is, indeed, the greatest of conquerors.

– Buddha

A winner is someone who recognises his God-given talents, works his tail off to develop them into skills and uses these skills to accomplish his goals.

– Larry Bird

Amateurs wait for inspiration. The rest of us just get up and go to work.

– Chuck Close

An expert is a person who has made all the mistakes that can be made, in a very narrow field.

– Niels Bohr

A rock pile ceases to be a rock pile the moment a single man contemplates it, bearing within him the image of a cathedral.

– Antoine de Saint-Exupéry

The longer we dwell on our misfortunes, the greater is their power to harm us.

– Voltaire

We must become the change we want to see.

– Mahatma Gandhi

Don't frown because you never know who is falling in love with your smile.

– Sin Vye St Tan

You were not born a winner, and you were not born a loser. You are what you make yourself be.

– Lou Holtz

What lies behind us and what lies before us are tiny matters compared to what lies within us.

– Walt Emerson

When you come to the end of your rope, tie a knot and hang on.

– Franklin D. Roosevelt

Our greatest glory is not in never failing, but in rising up every time we fail.

– Ralph Waldo Emerson

Vitality shows in not only the ability to persist but the ability to start over.

– F. Scott Fitzgerald

The drops of rain make a hole in the stone not by violence but by oft falling.

– Lucretius

It's not that I'm so smart, it's just that I stay with problems longer

– Albert Einstein

64

I Miss You Quotes

Being apart from the one you love can be a totally gut-wrenching affair. Here is a series of I miss you quotes to soothe your aching soul. Let some of these missing you quotes soothe your aching soul.

> A day without you is like a day without sunshine... I miss you...
>
> — ***Author Unknown***

> Absence diminishes little passions and increases great ones, as the wind extinguishes candles and fans a fire.
>
> — ***Francois Duc de la Rochefoucauld***

> Absence from whom we love is worse than death, and frustrates hope severer than despair.
>
> — ***William Cowper***

> Absence makes the heart grow fonder.
>
> — ***American Proverb***

> Can miles truly separate you from friends.... If you want to be with someone you love, aren't you already there?
>
> — ***Richard Bach***

> Every parting is a form of death, as every reunion is a type of heaven.
>
> — ***Tryon Edwards***

For everything you have missed, you have gained something else, and for everything you gain, you lose something else.

— Ralph Waldo Emerson

I keep coming back to you in my head, but you couldn't know that, and I have no carbons.

— Adrienne Rich

I miss you like the sun misses the flowers, like the sun misses the flowers in the depths of winter, instead of beauty to direct it's light to, the heart hardens like the frozen world which your absence has banished me to.

— William in "A Knight's Tale"

If I had a single flower for every time I think about you, I could walk forever in my garden.

— Claudia Ghandi

Life is so short, so fast the lone hours fly,

We ought to be together, you and I.

— Henry Alford

Love is missing someone whenever you're apart, but somehow feeling warm inside because you're close in heart.

— Kay Knudsen

Love reckons hours for months, and days for years; and every little absence is an age.

— John Dryden

Nothing makes the earth seem so spacious as to have friends at a distance; they make the latitudes and longitudes.

— Henry David Thoreau

Parting is all we know of heaven and all we need to know of hell.

— Emily Dickinson

Sometimes, when one person is missing, the whole world seems depopulated.

— Lamartine

The joy of meeting pays the pangs of absence; else who could bear it?

— Nicholas Rowe

The reason it hurts so much to separate is because our souls are connected.

— Nicholas Sparks

When I go away from you
The world beats dead
Like a slackened drum....

— Amy Lowell

What shall I do with all the days and hours
That must be counted ere I see thy face?
How shall I charm the interval that lowers
Between this time and that sweet time of grace?

— Frances Anne Kemble

When I miss you, I don't have to go far... I just have to look inside my heart because that's where I'll find you.

— Ruthie

When I miss you, sometimes I listen to music or look at pictures of you, not to remind me of you but to make me feel as if I'm with you. It makes me forget the distance and capture you.

— James

When the night has come
and the land is dark,
when the moon is the only light we'll see...
look at the stars;
can you count them?
I miss you that much.

— Laura

When you miss me just look up to the night sky and remember, I'm like a star; sometimes you can't see me, but I'm always there.

— Jayde

Where you used to be, there is a hole in the world, which I find myself constantly walking around in the daytime, and falling in at night. I miss you like hell.

— Edna St. Vincent Millay

Why is it that when you miss someone so much that your heart is ready to disintegrate, you hear the saddest song on the radio?

— Pete & Pete

Your absence has gone through me
Like thread through a needle
Everything I do is stitched with its colour.

— W.S. Merwin

65

Jawaharlal Nehru Quotes

Pandit Jawaharlal Nehru (1888-1964) was the first Prime Minister of India. He was highly instrumental in helping India gain independence from the British. One of the founders of modern India, he was also an important figure in the international politics of the post-war era. Throughout his life, Nehru was also an advocate for Fabian socialism and the public sector as the means by which long-standing challenges of economic development could be addressed by poorer nations. Here is a collection of meaningful quotes by Nehru.

A leader or a man of action in a crisis almost always acts subconsciously and then thinks of the reasons for his action.

A moment comes, which comes but rarely in history, when we step out from the old to the new; when an age ends; and when the soul of a nation long suppressed finds utterance.

A theory must be tempered with reality.

Action itself, so long as I am convinced that it is right action, gives me satisfaction.

Action to be effective must be directed to clearly conceived ends.

Citizenship consists in the service of the country.

Crises and deadlocks when they occur have at least this advantage, that they force us to think.

Culture is the widening of the mind and of the spirit.

Democracy and socialism are means to an end, not the end itself.

Democracy is good. I say this because other systems are worse.

Every little thing counts in a crisis.

Facts are facts and will not disappear on account of your likes.

Failure comes only when we forget our ideals and objectives and principles.

Great causes and little men go ill together.

I have become a queer mixture of the East and the West, out of place everywhere, at home nowhere.

Ignorance is always afraid of change.

It is only too easy to make suggestions and later try to escape the consequences of what we say.

It is the habit of every aggressor nation to claim that it is acting on the defensive.

Let us be a little humble; let us think that the truth may not perhaps be entirely with us.

Life is like a game of cards. The hand you are dealt is determinism; the way you play it is free will.

Loyal and efficient work in a great cause, even though it may not be immediately recognised, ultimately bears fruit.

Obviously, the highest type of efficiency is that which can utilise existing material to the best advantage.

Our chief defect is that we are more given to talking about things than to doing them.

Peace is not a relationship of nations. It is a condition of mind brought about by a serenity of soul. Peace is not merely the absence of war. It is also a state of mind. Lasting peace can come only to peaceful people.

Socialism is... not only a way of life, but a certain scientific approach to social and economic problems.

The art of a people is a true mirror to their minds.

The forces in a capitalist society, if left unchecked, tend to make the rich richer and the poor poorer.

The man who has gotten everything he wants is all in favor of peace and order.

The only alternative to coexistence is codestruction.

The person who runs away exposes himself to that very danger more than a person who sits quietly.

The person who talks most of his own virtue is often the least virtuous.

The policy of being too cautious is the greatest risk of all.

The purely agitational attitude is not good enough for a detailed consideration of a subject.

There is perhaps nothing so bad and so dangerous in life as fear.

Time is not measured by the passing of years but by what one does, what one feels, and what one achieves.

To be in good moral condition requires at least as much training as to be in good physical condition.

We live in a wonderful world that is full of beauty, charm and adventure. There is no end to the adventures that we can have if only we seek them with our eyes open.

Without peace, all other dreams vanish and are reduced to ashes.

You don't change the course of history by turning the faces of portraits to the wall.

66

Kindness Quotes

Many of us have been taught to be kind as a child. However in the business of daily living, somehow along the way some of us have lost touch with extending kindness to others. Recall when's the last time you've been kind to someone else. It usually didn't involve some big acts of sacrifice, but rather little acts kindness like opening a door for someone, throwing a stranger a cheerful smile, swallowing an unkind word, saying a sincere compliment. Yet kindness inevitably warms up the heart of both the giver and the recipient. Here is a collection that will cause you to stop and ponder on the greatness of simple acts of kindness.

A kind and compassionate act is often its own reward.

— ***William John Bennett***

A kind deed a day, like little drops of rain, Makes a mighty ocean and a gracious nation.

— ***Lin Hsiu Nei***

A kind heart is a fountain of gladness, making everything in its vicinity into smiles.

— ***Washington Irving***

A kind word is like a Spring day.

— ***Russian Proverb***

A word of kindness is seldom spoken in vain, while witty saying are as easily lost as the pearls slipping from a broken string.

— George D. Prentice

Be kind, for everyone you meet is fighting a harder battle.

— Plato

Beginning today, treat everyone you meet as if they were going to be dead by midnight. Extend to them all the care, kindness and understanding you can muster, and do it with no thought of any reward. Your life will never be the same again.

— Og Mandino

Constant kindness can accomplish much. As the sun makes ice melt, kindness causes misunderstanding, mistrust, and hostility to evaporate.

— Albert Schweitzer

Have you had a kindness shown?
Pass it on;
'Twas not given for thee alone,
Pass it on;
Let it travel down the years,
Let it wipe another's tears,
Till in Heaven the deed appears,
Pass it on.

— Henry Burton

How far you go in life depends on you being tender with the young, compassionate with the aged, sympathetic with the striving and tolerant of the weak and the strong. Because someday in life, you will have been all of these.

— George Washington Carver

I expect to pass through this world but once. Any good, therefore, that I can do or any kindness I can show to any fellow creature, let me do it now. Let me not defer or neglect it for I shall not pass this way again.

— Stephen Grellet

If we cannot be clever, we can always be kind.

— Alfred Fripp

Kind words can be short and easy to speak, but their echoes are truly endless.

— Mother Teresa

Kindness gives birth to kindness.

— Sophocles

Kindness is an inner desire that makes us want to do good things even if we do not get anything in return. It is the joy of our life to do them. When we do good things from this inner desire, there is kindness in everything we think, say, want, and do.

— Emanuel Swedenborg

Kindness is more than deeds. It is an attitude, an expression, a look, a touch. It is anything that lifts another person.

— C. Neil Strait

Kindness is tenderness. Kindness is love, but perhaps greater than love...Kindness is good will. Kindness says, "I want you to be happy."

— Randolph Ray

Kindness is the language which the deaf can hear and the blind can see.

— Mark Twain

Kindness in words creates confidence. Kindness in thinking creates profoundness. Kindness in giving creates love.

— Lao Tzu

Let no one ever come to you without leaving better and happier. Be the living expression of God's kindness: kindness in your face, kindness in your eyes, kindness in your smile.

— Mother Teresa

Love and kindness are never wasted. They always make a difference.

— ***Barbara DeAngelis***

Never look down on anybody unless you're helping him up.

— ***Jesse Jackson***

No act of kindness, no matter how small, is ever wasted.

— ***Aesop***

Of all the ways you can think of, none has a sixteenth part of the value of loving kindness. Loving kindness is a freedom of the heart which takes in all the ways. It is luminous, shining, blazing forth.

— ***Itivuttaka Sutta***

Once you begin to acknowledge random acts of kindness—both the ones you have received and the ones you have given—you can no longer believe that what you do does not matter.

— ***Dawna Markova***

One can never pay in gratitude: one can only pay "in kind" somewhere else in life.

— ***Anne Morrow Lindbergh***

One who knows how to show and to accept kindness will be a friend better than any possession.

— ***Sophocles***

Remember there's no such thing as a small act of kindness. Every act creates a ripple with no logical end.

— ***Scott Adams***

Tenderness and kindness are not signs of weakness and despair, but manifestations of strength and resolution.

— ***Kahlil Gibran***

The centre of human nature is rooted in ten thousand ordinary acts of kindness that define our days.

— ***Stephen Jay Gould***

The flower of kindness will grow. Maybe not now, but it will some day. And in kind that kindness will flow, for kindness grows in this way.

– Robert Alan

The ideas that have lighted my way have been kindness, beauty and truth.

– Albert Einstein

The truest greatness lies in being kind, the truest wisdom in a happy mind.

– Ella Wheeler Wilcox

Those who bring sunshine to the lives of others cannot keep it from themselves.

– James Matthew Barrie

Three things in human life are important. The first is to be kind. The second is to be kind. And the third is to be kind.

– Henry James

To cultivate kindness is a valuable part of the business of life.

– Samuel Johnson

Today I bent the truth to be kind, and I have no regret, for I am far surer of what is kind than I am of what is true.

– Robert Brault

When I was young, I admired clever people. Now that I am old, I admire kind people.

– Abraham Joshua Heschel

When we feel love and kindness toward others, it not only makes others feel loved and cared for, but it helps us also to develop inner happiness and peace.

– Dalai Lama

When you are kind to others, it not only changes you, it changes the world.

– Harold Kushner

When you are kind to someone in trouble, you hope they'll remember and be kind to someone else. And it'll become like wildfire.

– Whoopi Goldberg

When you carry out acts of kindness you get a wonderful feeling inside. It is as though something inside your body responds and says, yes, this is how I ought to feel.

– Harold Kushner

You can accomplish by kindness what you cannot by force.

– Publilius Syrus

You cannot do a kindness too soon, for you never know how soon it will be too late.

– Ralph Waldo Emerson

67

Leadership Quotes

Leaders aren't only found in corporate or military environments. Even at homes, we can become "leaders" to other family members or the kids. As long as we are dealing and interacting with people, there's plenty of chances for us to take on the role of leadership. These quotes are great be it that you are the manager of a big department or the mother of five children. You are put into the leadership role. Whether you want to learn to become a good or even a great leader, the choice is up to you.

May these quotes inspire you!

A leader is a dealer in hope.

– Napoleon Bonaparte

A leader is one who knows the way, goes the way and shows the way.

– John C. Maxwell

A leader must have the courage to act against an expert's advice.

– James Callaghan

A leader, once convinced that a particular course of action is the right one, must be undaunted when the going gets tough.

– Ronald Reagan

A leader takes people where they want to go. A great leader takes people where they don't necessarily want to go, but ought to be.

— Rosalynn Carter

A new leader has to be able to change an organisation that is dreamless, soulless and visionless... someone's got to make a wake up call.

— Warren Bennis

All Leadership is influence.

— John C. Maxwell

An empowered organisation is one in which individuals have the knowledge, skill, desire, and opportunity to personally succeed in a way that leads to collective organisational success.

— Stephen R. Covey

Before you are a leader, success is all about growing yourself. When you become a leader, success is all about growing others.

— Jack Welch

Delegating work works, provided the one delegating works, too.

— Robert Half

Don't tell people how to do things, tell them what to do and let them surprise you with their results.

— George S. Patton

Effective leadership is putting first things first. Effective management is discipline, carrying it out.

— Stephen Covey

Great leaders are almost always great simplifiers, who can cut through argument, debate, and doubt to offer a solution everybody can understand.

— General Colin Powell

Lead and inspire people. Don't try to manage and manipulate people. Inventories can be managed but people must be lead.

— Ross Perot

Leadership cannot really be taught. It can only be learned.

— Harold Geneen

Leadership is based on a spiritual quality; the power to inspire others to follow.

— Vincent Lombardi

Leadership is doing what is right when no one is watching.

— George Van Valkenburg

Leadership is the challenge to be something more than average.

— Jim Rohn

Leadership is the art of getting someone else to do something you want done because he wants to do it.

— Dwight Eisenhower

Management is doing things right; leadership is doing the right things.

— Peter F. Drucker

My own definition of leadership is this: The capacity and the will to rally men and women to a common purpose and the character which inspires confidence.

— General Montgomery

The best executive is the one who has sense enough to pick good men to do what he wants done, and self-restraint to keep from meddling with them while they do it.

— Theodore Roosevelt

The great leaders are like the best conductors—they reach beyond the notes to reach the magic in the players.

— Blaine Lee

The leader is one who mobilises others toward a goal shared by leaders and followers.... Leaders, followers and goals make up the three equally necessary supports for leadership.

— Gary Wills

The leadership instinct you are born with is the backbone. You develop the funny bone and the wishbone that go with it.

— Elaine Agather

The quality of a leader is reflected in the standards they set for themselves.

— Ray Kroc

The secret of a leader lies in the tests he has faced over the whole course of his life and the habit of action he develops in meeting those tests.

— Gail Sheehy

The task of leadership is not to put greatness into people, but to elicit it, for the greatness is there already.

— John Buchan

The task of the leader is to get his people from where they are to where they have not been.

— Henry Kissinger

The very essence of leadership is that you have to have vision. You can't blow an uncertain trumpet.

— Theodore M. Hesburgh

Treat people as if they were what they ought to be and you help them to become what they are capable of being.

— Johann Wolfgang Von Goethe

68

Letting Go Quotes

In life, there is many things that we have to learn to let go. We have to let go of situations, things, memories, people and even ourselves. It's easy to form an attachment to people and things. When you've formed an attachment to people and things, it can be a very painful experience and feeling when you realised that it's time to let go. Even the mere thought of not having that person or thing in your life just squeeses your heart in pain. Letting go is one of the hardest lessons in life. Here is a collection of letting go quotes that will give you some hope and words of encouragement during those challenging times.

> All the art of living lies in a fine mingling of letting go and holding on.
>
> — ***Havelock Ellis***

> As I started to picture the trees in the storm, the answer began to dawn on me. The trees in the storm don't try to stand up straight and tall and erect. They allow themselves to bend and be blown with the wind. They understand the power of letting go. Those trees and those branches that try too hard to stand up strong and straight are the ones that break. Now is not the time for you to be strong, Julia, or you, too, will break.
>
> — ***Julia Butterfly Hill***

Breathe. Let go. And remind yourself that this very moment is the only one you know you have for sure.

— Oprah Winfrey

By letting it go it all gets done. The world is won by those who let it go. But when you try and try. The world is beyond the winning.

— Lao Tzu

Courage is the power to let go of the familiar.

— Raymond Lindquist

Creativity can be described as letting go of certainties,

— Gail Sheehy

Hanging onto resentment is letting someone you despise live rent-free in your head.

— Ann Landers

Inner peace can be reached only when we practice forgiveness. Forgiveness is letting go of the past, and is therefore the means for correcting our misperceptions.

— Gerald Jampolsky

Let go. Why do you cling to pain? There is nothing you can do about the wrongs of yesterday. It is not yours to judge. Why hold on to the very thing which keeps you from hope and love?

— Leo Buscaglia

Letting go doesn't mean giving up, but rather accepting that there are things that cannot be.

— Anon

Loving someone is setting them free, letting them go.

— Kate Winslet

People have a hard time letting go of their suffering. Out of a fear of the unknown, they prefer suffering that is familiar.

— Thich Nhat Hanh

Some think it's holding on that makes one strong; sometimes it's letting go.

— Sylvia Robinson

Sometimes being a friend means mastering the art of timing. There is a time for silence. A time to let go and allow people to hurl themselves into their own destiny. And a time to prepare to pick up the pieces when it's all over.

– Gloria Naylor

Stand up and walk out of your history.

– Phil McGraw

The harder you fight to hold on to specific assumptions, the more likely there's gold in letting go of them.

– John Seely Brown

Think about any attachments that are depleting your emotional reserves. Consider letting them go.

– Oprah Winfrey

Truly loving another means letting go of all expectations. It means full acceptance, even celebration of another's personhood.

– Karen Casey

We must be willing to let go of the life we have planned, so as to accept the life that is waiting for us.

– Joseph Campbell

When I let go of what I am, I become what I might be.

– Lao Tzu

You have been warned against letting the golden hours slip by. Yes, but some of them are golden only because we let them slip by.

– James Matthew Barrie

69

Life Quotes

Life is really short and instead of being burdened by the heavy "shoulds" and "could have beens", perhaps it's really time to have the courage to make more mistakes, be sillier, and travel lighter for the rest of your life. We only live once. During the down days, if you choose to keep in mind that you probably have more chances than others, more things to be thankful for than others, and more time to live on this Earth than others, you'd be reminded that your life is indeed very precious. There is many people who are grateful for you and you might not realise about that. Life needs you and that's because life has given you a path that only you can travel, and no one else will do. Here is a collection of life quotes.

All life is an experiment.

— *Ralph Waldo Emerson*

All the art of living lies in a fine mingling of letting go and holding on.

— *Havelock Ellis*

Be glad of life because it gives you the chance to love and to work and to play and to look up at the stars.

— *Henry Van Dyke*

Believe that life is worth living and your belief will help create the fact.

— *William James*

Don't take life too seriously. You'll never get out alive.

— ***Bugs Bunny***

Don't cry because its over, smile because it happened.

— ***Dr. Seuss***

Every passing minute is another chance to turn it all around.

— ***From Vanilla Sky***

Few of us write great novels; all of us live them.

— ***Mignon McLaughlin***

Finish each day and be done with it. You have done what you could; some blunders and absurdities have crept in; forget them as soon as you can. Tomorrow is a new day; you shall begin it serenely and with too high a spirit to be encumbered with your old nonsense.

— ***Ralph Waldo Emerson***

For a long time it had seemed to me that life was about to begin—real life. But there was always some obstacle in the way, something to be gotten through first, some unfinished business, time still to be served, a debt to be paid. Then life would begin. At last it dawned on me that these obstacles were my life.

— ***Alfred D. Souza***

He who has a why to live can bear almost any how.

— ***Friedrich Nietzsche***

Here is the test to find whether your mission on earth is finished. If you're alive, it isn't.

— ***Richard Bach***

How we spend our days is, of course, how we spend our lives.

— ***Annie Dillard***

I arise in the morning torn between a desire to improve the world and a desire to enjoy the world. This makes it hard to plan the day.

— ***Elwyn Brooks White***

I count life just a stuff

To try the soul's strength on.

— Robert Browning

In three words I can sum up everything I've learned about life. It goes on.

— Robert Frost

It is not length of life, but depth of life.

— Ralph Waldo Emerson

Learn as if you were going to live forever. Live as if you were going to die tomorrow.

— Mahatma Gandhi

Let us be greateful to people who make us happy, they are the charming gardeners who make our souls blossom.

— Marcel Proust

Life does not cease to be funny when people die any more than it ceases to be serious when people laugh.

— George Bernard Shaw

Life is a ticket to the greatest show on earth.

— Martin H. Fischer

Life is an opportunity, benefit from it. Life is beauty, admire it.

Life is bliss, taste it. Life is a dream, realise it.

Life is a challenge, meet it. Life is a duty, complete it.

Life is a game, play it. Life is a promise, fulfil it.

Life is sorrow, overcome it. Life is a song, sing it.

Life is a struggle, accept it. Life is a tragedy, confront it.

Life is an adventure, dare it. Life is luck, make it.

Life is too precious, do not destroy it. Life is life, fight for it.

— Mother Teresa

Life is just a chance to grow a soul.

— A. Powell Davies

Life is like a hot bath. It feels good while you're in it, but the longer you stay in, the more wrinkled you get.

— ***Robbert Oustin***

Life is like dancing. If we have a big floor, many people will dance. Some will get angry when the rhythm changes. But life is changing all the time.

— ***Don Miguel Ruiz***

Life should not be a journey to the grave with the intention of arriving safely in an attractive and well preserved body, but rather to skid in sideways, champagne in one hand—strawberries in the other, body thoroughly used up, totally worn out and screaming "WOOHOO—What a Ride!"

— ***Attributed to an octogenarian named Mavis Leyrer, of Seattle***

Life is rather like a tin of sardines—we're all of us looking for the key.

— ***Alan Bennett***

Life is the sum of all your choices.

— ***Albert Camus***

Life is what we make it, always has been, always will be.

— ***Grandma Moses***

Live with no excuses and love with no regrets.

— ***Montel***

Look, I don't want to wax philosophic, but I will say that if you're alive you've got to flap your arms and legs, you've got to jump around a lot, for life is the very opposite of death, and therefore you must at very least think noisy and colourfully, or you're not alive.

— ***Mel Brooks***

May you live every day of your life.

— ***Jonathan Swift***

My formula for living is quite simple. I get up in the morning and I go to bed at night. In between, I occupy myself as best I can.

— ***Cary Grant***

Nobody grows old merely by living a number of years. We grow old by deserting our ideals. Years may wrinkle the skin, but to give up enthusiasm wrinkles the soul.

— Samuel Ullman

Only a few things are really important.

— Marie Dressler

Our greatest glory is not in never falling, but in rising every time we fall.

— Confucius

Our lives are like a candle in the wind.

— Carl Sandburg

The first step to getting the things you want out of life is this: Decide what you want.

— Ben Stein

The great use of life is to spend it for something that will outlast it.

— William James

The price of anything is the amount of life you exchange for it.

— Henry David Thoreau

The purpose of life is a life of purpose.

— Robert Byrne

The question in life is not whether you get knocked down. You will. The question is, are you ready to get back up.. and fight for what you believe in.

— Dan Quayle

There are only two ways to live your life. One is as though nothing is a miracle. The other is as if everything is.

— Albert Einstein

This life is yours. Take the power to choose what you want to do and do it well. Take the power to love what you want in life and love it honestly. Take the power to walk in the forest and be a part of nature. Take the power to control your own life. No one else can do it for you. Take the power to make your life happy.

— Susan Polis Schutz

Time is the coin of your life. It is the only coin you have, and only you can determine how it will be spent. Be careful lest you let other people spend it for you.

— Carl Sandburg

To live is so startling it leaves little time for anything else.

— Emily Dickinson

To live remains an art which everyone must learn, and which no one can teach.

— Havelock Ellis

We act as though comfort and luxury were the chief requirements of life, when all that we need to make us happy is something to be enthusiastic about.

— Albert Einstein

What is life? It is the flash of a firefly in the night. It is the breath of a buffalo in the wintertime. It is the little shadow which runs across the grass and loses itself in the sunset.

— Crowfoot

What you leave behind is not what is engraved in stone monuments, but what is woven into the lives of others.

— Pericles

When everything seems to be going against you, remember that the airplane takes off against the wind, not with it.

— Henry Ford

When you come to the end of your rope, tie a knot and hang on.

— Franklin D. Roosevelt

You cannot discover the purpose of life by asking someone else—the only way you'll ever get the right answer is by asking yourself.

— Terri Guillemets

You must be the change you wish to see in the world.

— Mahatma Gandhi

You only live once—but if you work it right, once is enough.

— Joe E. Lewis

Your life lies before you like a path of driven snow, be careful how you tread it cause every step will show.

— Lowri Williams

70

Mahatma Gandhi Quotes

Mohandas Karamchand Gandhi who was born on October 2, 1869, died as the *Mahatma* on January 30, 1948. The man who came to be regarded as the symbol of independent India was greatly revered by his own countrymen. Indians came to call him Mahatma or "the Great Soul." A large number of famous Gandhi quotes contain so much wisdom that they have gained immortality. These famous Gandhi quotes reveal the wisdom of this great man.

Strength does not come from physical capacity. It comes from an indomitable will.

Whenever you are confronted with an opponent, conquer him with love.

A 'No' uttered from the deepest conviction is better than a 'Yes' merely uttered to please, or worse, to avoid trouble.

A coward is incapable of exhibiting love; it is the prerogative of the brave.

A religion that takes no account of practical affairs and does not help to solve them is no religion.

Adaptability is not imitation. It means power of resistance and assimilation.

Anger and intolerance are the twin enemies of correct understanding.

You can chain me, you can torture me, you can even destroy this body, but you will never imprison my mind.

Culture of the mind must be subservient to the heart

It is better to be violent, if there is violence in our hearts, than to put on the cloak of nonviolence to cover impotence.

Happiness is when what you think, what you say, and what you do are in harmony.

The weak can never forgive. Forgiveness is the attribute of the strong.

Hate the sin, love the sinner.

I want freedom for the full expression of my personality.

Victory attained by violence is tantamount to a defeat, for it is momentary.

Freedom is not worth having if it does not include the freedom to make mistakes.

Live as if you were to die tomorrow. Learn as if you were to live forever.

Permanent good can never be the outcome of untruth and violence.

There is nothing that wastes the body like worry, and one who has any faith in God should be ashamed to worry about anything whatsoever

I like your Christ, I do not like your Christians. Your Christians are so unlike your Christ.

Nobody can hurt me without my permission.

71

Mark Twain Quotes

Born as Samuel Langhorne Clemens, he is better known by his pen name Mark Twain. Besides being famous for his novels, Adventures of Huckleberry Finn and The Adventures of Tom Sawyer, he is known for his great quotations too. Below is a selection of some of his best quotations. Most are very witty and clearly show Mark Twain as the popular humorist and satirist he was.

A banker is a fellow who lends you his umbrella when the sun is shining, but wants it back the minute it begins to rain.

A man's character may be learned from the adjectives which he habitually uses in conversation.

A person with a new idea is a crank until the idea succeeds.

Always acknowledge a fault. This will throw those in authority off their guard and give you an opportunity to commit more.

Always do right. This will gratify some people and astonish the rest.

Age is an issue of mind over matter. If you don't mind, it doesn't matter.

Anger is an acid that can do more harm to the vessel in which it is stored than to anything on which it is poured.

Be careful about reading health books. You may die of a misprint.

Be careless in your dress if you will, but keep a tidy soul.

Buy land, they're not making it anymore.

Clothes make the man. Naked people have little or no influence on society.

Courage is resistance to fear, mastery of fear—not absence of fear.

Don't go around saying the world owes you a living. The world owes you nothing. It was here first.

Drag your thoughts away from your troubles... by the ears, by the heels, or any other way you can manage it.

Grief can take care of itself, but to get the full value of a joy you must have somebody to divide it with.

Habit is habit and not to be flung out of the window by any man, but coaxed downstairs a step at a time.

I can live for two months on a good compliment.

I have been through some terrible things in my life, some of which actually happened.

I have never let my schooling interfere with my education.

I was gratified to be able to answer promptly. I said I don't know.

If you tell the truth you don't have to remember anything.

It is better to deserve honours and not have them than to have them and not to deserve them.

It is better to keep your mouth closed and let people think you are a fool than to open it and remove all doubt.

It is curious that physical courage should be so common in the world and moral courage so rare.

It usually takes more than three weeks to prepare a good impromptu speech.

Keep away from people who try to belittle your ambitions. Small people always do that, but the really great make you feel that you, too, can become great.

Let us so live that when we come to die even the undertaker will be sorry.

Life would be infinitely happier if we could only be born at the age of eighty and gradually approach eighteen.

Many a small thing has been made large by the right kind of advertising.

Name the greatest of all inventors. Accident.

The best way to cheer yourself is to try to cheer someone else up.

The human race has one really effective weapon, and that is laughter.

The man who doesn't read good books has no advantage over the man who can't read them.

Time cools, time clarifies; no mood can be maintained quite unaltered through the course of hours.

72

Mistake Quotes

Some said that people who fear to make mistakes hardly do anything with their lives. But failure to learn from one's mistakes will lead one to commit the same mistake again. There is got to be a balance somewhere. To make a mistake is human. Let this collection of mistake quotes highlights the importance of learning from one's mistakes and moving forward.

A life spent making mistakes is not only more honourable, but more useful than a life spent doing nothing.

— *George Bernard Shaw*

Admit your errors before someone else exaggerates them.

— *Andrew V. Mason*

After all these years, I am still involved in the process of self-discovery. It's better to explore life and make mistakes than to play it safe. Mistakes are part of the dues one pays for a full life.

— *Sophia Loren*

An expert is a person who has made all the mistakes that can be made in a very narrow field.

— *Niels Bohr*

Any fool can try to defend his mistakes—and most fools do—but it gives one a feeling of nobility to admit one's mistakes. By fighting, you never get enough, but by yielding, you get more than you expected.

— Lawrence G. Lovasik

As long as the world is turning and spinning, we're gonna be dizzy and we're gonna make mistakes.

— Mel Brooks

As you begin to take action toward the fulfilment of your goals and dreams, you must realise that not every action will be perfect. Not every action will produce the desired result. Not every action will work. Making mistakes, getting it almost right, and experimenting to see what happens are all part of the process of eventually getting it right.

— Jack Canfield

Assert your right to make a few mistakes. If people can't accept your imperfections, that's their fault.

— Dr. David M. Burns

Be thankful for your mistakes. They will teach you valuable lessons.

— Author Unknown

Constant effort and frequent mistakes are the stepping stones of genius.

— Elbert Hubbard

Creativity is allowing yourself to make mistakes. Art is knowing which ones to keep.

— Scott Adams

Don't argue for other people's weaknesses. Don't argue for your own. When you make a mistake, admit it, correct it, and learn from it—immediately.

— Stephen Covey

Experience is that marvelous thing that enables you to recognise a mistake when you make it again.

— Franklin P. Jones

I have learned throughout my life as a composer chiefly through my mistakes and pursuits of false assumptions, not by my exposure to founts of wisdom and knowledge.

— Igor Stravinsky

I have to say I've made many mistakes, and been humbled many, many times. But you know what? It's never too late to learn.

– Kathy Ireland

If I had to live my life again, I'd make the same mistakes, only sooner.

– Tallulah Bankhead

If I had my life to live over... I'd dare to make more mistakes next time.

– Nadine Stair

If you don't make mistakes, you're not working on hard enough problems. And that's a big mistake.

– F. Wikzek

If you have made mistakes, even serious ones, there is always another chance for you. What we call failure is not the falling down but the staying down.

– Mary Pickford

If you're not making mistakes, you're not taking risks, and that means you're not going anywhere. The key is to make mistakes faster than the competition, so you have more changes to learn and win.

– John W. Holt, Jr.

In the game of life it's a good idea to have a few early losses, which relieves you of the pressure of trying to maintain an undefeated season.

– Bill Vaughan

It is a mistake to look too far ahead. Only one link in the chain of destiny can be handled at a time.

– Winston Churchill

It was when I found out I could make mistakes that I knew I was on to something.

– Ornette Coleman

It's always helpful to learn from your mistakes because then your mistakes seem worthwhile.

– Garry Marshall

Laughing at our mistakes can lengthen our own life. Laughing at someone else's can shorten it.

— Cullen Hightower

Making mistakes simply means you are learning faster.

— Weston H. Agor

Mistakes are a part of being human. Appreciate your mistakes for what they are: precious life lessons that can only be learned the hard way. Unless it's a fatal mistake, which, at least, others can learn from.

— Al Franken

Mistakes are painful when they happen, but years later a collection of mistakes is what is called experience.

— Denis Waitley

Mistakes are the portals of discovery.

— James Joyce

Mistakes, obviously, show us what needs improving. Without mistakes, how would we know what we had to work on?

— Peter McWilliams

Nowadays most people die of a sort of creeping common sense, and discover when it is too late that the only things one never regrets are one's mistakes.

— Oscar Wilde

"Picking up the pieces when they fall" begins a journey to living anew with love, courage, and hope for a bright future.

— Steve Brunkhorst

Preparation for success means that any failure you meet is seen as an opportunity to learn from mistakes. Remember that failure is your best teacher.

— Byron Pulsifer

Punishing honest mistakes stifles creativity. I want people moving and shaking the earth and they're going to make mistakes.

— Ross Perot

She had an unequalled gift... of squeezing big mistakes into small opportunities.

— Henry James

Success seems to be connected with action. Successful people keep moving. They make mistakes, but they don't quit.

— Conrad Hilton

The biggest mistake people make in life is not trying to make a living at doing what they most enjoy.

— Malcolm S. Forbes

The difference between greatness and mediocrity is often how an individual views a mistake.

— Nelson Boswell

The greatest mistake you can make in life is to be continually fearing you will make one.

— Elbert Hubbard

The man who achieves makes many mistakes, but he never makes the biggest mistake of all—doing nothing.

— Benjamin Franklin

The man who makes no mistakes does not usually make anything.

— William Connor Magee

The only real mistake is the one from which we learn nothing.

— John Powell

The price of inaction is far greater than the cost of making a mistake.

— Meister Eckhart

There is a certain degree of satisfaction in having the courage to admit one's errors. It not only clears up the air of guilt and defensiveness, but often helps solve the problem created by the error.

— Dale Carnegie

To avoid situations in which you might make mistakes may be the biggest mistake of all.

— Peter McWilliams

When you make a mistake, admit it. If you don't, you only make matters worse.

— Ward Cleaver

When you make a mistake, don't look back at it long. Take the reason of the thing into your mind and then look forward. Mistakes are lessons of wisdom. The past cannot be changed. The future is yet in your power.

— Hugh White

Whenever you make a mistake or get knocked down by life, don't look back at it too long. Mistakes are life's way of teaching you. Your capacity for occasional blunders is inseparable from your capacity to reach your goals.

— Og Mandino

While one person hesitates because he feels inferior, the other is busy making mistakes and becoming superior.

— Henry C. Link

Your mistake does not define who you are...you are your possibilities.

— Oprah Winfrey

73

Mother Teresa Quotes

Born as Agnesa Gonxha Bojaxhiu (1910-1997), Mother Teresa was a Roman Catholic nun of Albanian descent. She founded the Missionaries of Charity in India. Her work among the poverty-stricken of Kolkata made her one of the most well-known people in the world. She was also sometimes referred to as the "Angel of Mercy" and "Saint of the Gutter" by her supporters. She is a remarkable woman and her wisdom will speak to your heart. Here is a collection of some of the best quotes by Mother Teresa. You may find great inspiration and humility from these quotes.

> Be faithful in small things because it is in them that your strength lies.
>
> Do not think that love, in order to be genuine, has to be extraordinary. What we need is to love without getting tired.
>
> Do not wait for leaders; do it alone, person to person.
>
> Everytime you smile at someone, it is an action of love, a gift to that person, a beautiful thing.
>
> Good works are links that form a chain of love.
>
> If we want a love message to be heard, it has got to be sent out. To keep a lamp burning, we have to keep putting oil in it.

If you can't feed a hundred people, then feed just one.

Intense love does not measure, it just gives.

It is a kingly act to assist the fallen.

In this life we cannot do great things. We can only do small things with great love.

It is not the magnitude of our actions but the amount of love that is put into them that matters.

Kind words can be short and easy to speak, but their echoes are truly endless.

Let us always meet each other with smile, for the smile is the beginning of love.

Let us not be satisfied with just giving money. Money is not enough, money can be got, but they need your hearts to love them. So, spread your love everywhere you go.

Love begins at home, and it is not how much we do... but how much love we put in that action.

Love is a fruit in season at all times, and within reach of every hand.

The success of love is in the loving—it is not in the result of loving. Of course it is natural in love to want the best for the other person, but whether it turns out that way or not does not determine the value of what we have done.

We can do no great things, only small things with great love.

We ourselves feel that what we are doing is just a drop in the ocean. But the ocean would be less because of that missing drop.

We think sometimes that poverty is only being hungry, naked and homeless. The poverty of being unwanted, unloved and uncared for is the greatest poverty. We must start in our own homes to remedy this kind of poverty.

74

Mother Quotes

Mothers are a very special breed of people. Mother quotes are here to uplift your spirits as a mother to your children. These mother quotations are also terrific as mother's day quotes. Use these wonderful quotes to express your heartfelt loving thoughts about motherhood or to your own mother.

A man loves his sweetheart the most, his wife the best, but his mother the longest.

— ***Irish Proverb***

A mother is a person who seeing there are only four pieces of pie for five people, promptly announces she never did care for pie.

— ***Tenneva Jordan***

A mother is the truest friend we have, when trials heavy and sudden, fall upon us; when adversity takes the place of prosperity; when friends who rejoice with us in our sunshine desert us; when trouble thickens around us, still will she cling to us, and endeavor by her kind precepts and counsels to dissipate the clouds of darkness, and cause peace to return to our hearts.

— ***Washington Irving***

A mother understands what a child does not say.

— ***Jewish proverb***

A mother's arms are made of tenderness and children sleep soundly in them.

— Victor Hugo

A mother's love for her child is like nothing else in the world. It knows no law, no pity, it dares all things and crushes down remorselessly all that stands in its path.

— Agatha Christie

A mother's love liberates.

— Maya Angelou

A mother,

There to support you,

And hold you up whenever you need her.

— Laurel Stephens

All mothers are working mothers.

— Author Unknown

All that I am or hope to be, I owe to my angel mother.

— Abraham Lincoln

And so our mothers and grandmothers have, more often than not anonymously, handed on the creative spark, the seed of the flower they themselves never hoped to see — or like a sealed letter they could not plainly read.

— Alice Walker

Any mother could perform the jobs of several air traffic controllers with ease.

— Lisa Alther

Because I feel that in the heavens above
The angels, whispering one to another,
Can find among their burning tears of love,
None so devotional as that of "Mother,"
Therefore, by that dear name I have long called you,
You who are more than mother unto me.

— Edgar Allan Poe

Before becoming a mother I had a hundred theories on how to bring up children. Now I have seven children and only one theory: Love them, especially when they least deserve to be loved.

— *Kate Samperi*

Being a full-time mother is one of the highest salaried jobs in my field, since the payment is pure love.

— *Mildred B. Vermont*

Children and mothers never truly part -
Bound in the beating of each other's heart.

— *Charlotte Gray*

Education commences at the mother's knee, and every word spoken within the hearing of little children tends towards the formation of character.

— *Hosea Ballou*

Everybody wants to save the earth; nobody wants to help Mom with the dishes.

— *P.J. O'Rourke*

God could not be everywhere, so he created mothers.

— *Jewish Proverb*

Grown don't mean nothing to a mother. A child is a child. They get bigger, older, but grown? What's that suppose to mean? In my heart it don't mean a thing.

— *Toni Morrison*

I know how to do anything—I'm a mom.

— *Rosanne Barr*

I miss thee, my Mother! Thy image is still The deepest impressed on my heart.

— *Eliza Cook*

I never knew how much love my heart could hold until someone called me "mommy."

— *Author Unknown*

I think, at a child's birth, if a mother could ask a fairy godmother to endow it with the most useful gift, that gift would be curiosity.

— *Eleanor Roosevelt*

I thought my mom's whole purpose was to be my mom. That's how she made me feel.

— ***Natasha Gregson Wagner***

It is not until you become a mother that your judgement slowly turns to compassion and understanding.

— ***Erma Bombeck***

"M" is for the million things she gave me,
"O" means only that she's growing old,
"T" is for the tears she shed to save me,"H" is for her heart of purest gold;
"E" is for her eyes, with love-light shining,
"R" means right, and right she'll always be,
Put them all together, they spell "MOTHER,"
A word that means the world to me.

— ***Howard Johnson***

Most of all the other beautiful things in life come by twos and threes, by dozens and hundreds. Plenty of roses, stars, sunsets, rainbows, brothers and sisters, aunts and cousins, comrades and friends—but only one mother in the whole world.

— ***Kate Douglas Wiggin***

Mother is the name for God in the lips and hearts of little children.

— ***William Makepeace Thackeray***

Mother love is the fuel that enables a normal human being to do the impossible.

— ***Marion C. Garretty***

Mother—that was the bank where we deposited all our hurts and worries.

— ***T. DeWitt Talmage***

Mother's love grows by giving.

— ***Charles Lamb***

Mother's love is peace. It need not be acquired, it need not be deserved.

— ***Erich Fromm***

Motherhood has a very humanising effect. Everything gets reduced to essentials.

— ***Meryl Streep***

Motherhood is not for the faint-hearted. Frogs, skinned knees, and the insults of teenage girls are not meant for the wimpy.

— ***Danielle Steel***

My mother had a slender, small body, but a large heart—a heart so large that everybody's joys found welcome in it, and hospitable accommodation.

— ***Mark Twain***

My mother is a poem
I'll never be able to write,
though everything I write
is a poem to my mother.

— ***Sharon Doubiago***

My mother is my root, my foundation. She planted the seed that I base my life on, and that is the belief that the ability to achieve starts in your mind.

— ***Michael Jordan***

No matter how old a mother is, she watches her middle-aged children for signs of improvement.

— ***Florida Scott-Maxwell***

Now, as always, the most automated appliance in a household is the mother.

— ***Beverly Jones***

One good mother is worth a hundred schoolmasters.

— ***George Herbert***

She never quite leaves her children at home, even when she doesn't take them along.

— ***Margaret Culkin Banning***

She was of the stuff of which great men's mothers are made. She was indispensable to high generation, hated at tea parties, feared in shops, and loved at crises.

— ***Thomas Hardy***

Some mothers are kissing mothers and some are scolding mothers, but it is love just the same, and most mothers kiss and scold together.

— Pearl S. Buck

The heart of a mother is a deep abyss at the bottom of which you will always find forgiveness.

— Honoré de Balzac

The moment a child is born, the mother is also born. She never existed before. The woman existed, but the mother, never. A mother is something absolutely new.

— Rajneesh

The mother's heart is the child's school-room.

— Henry Ward Beecher

The strength of motherhood is greater than natural laws.

— Barbara Kingsolver

The sweetest sounds to mortals given
Are heard in Mother, Home, and Heaven.

— William Goldsmith Brown

There is only one pretty child in the world, and every mother has it.

— Chinese Proverb

When I was a child, my mother said to me, 'If you become a soldier, you'll be a general. If you become a monk you'll end up as the Pope.' Instead I became a painter and wound up as Picasso.

— Pablo Picasso

When you are a mother, you are never really alone in your thoughts. A mother always has to think twice, once for herself and once for her child.

— Sophia Loren

Who ran to help me when I fell,
And would some pretty story tell,
Or kiss the place to make it well?
My mother.

— Ann Taylor

Women do not have to sacrifice personhood if they are mothers. They do not have to sacrifice motherhood in order to be persons. Liberation was meant to expand women's opportunities, not to limit them. The self-esteem that has been found in new pursuits can also be found in mothering.

— *Elaine Heffner*

Women know The way to rear up children (to be just)
They know a simple, merry, tender knack
Of tying sashes, fitting baby shoes,
And stringing pretty words that make no sense,
And kissing full sense into empty words.

— *Elizabeth Barrett Browning*

Women who miscalculate are called mothers.

— *Abigail Van Buren*

You may have tangible wealth untold;
Caskets of jewels and coffers of gold.
Richer than I you can never be
I had a mother who read to me.

— *Strickland Gillilan*

Youth fades; love droops; the leaves of friendship fall; A mother's secret hope outlives them all.

— *Oliver Wendell Holmes*

75

Opportunity Quotes

Opportunity knocks but once. Do you make the most of your opportunities? Or do you dilly-dally and waste precious opportunities? If you procrastinate when opportunity knocks, you will suffer great loss. These inspirational opportunity quotes inspire us to make the most of every moment. Act fast, and act decisively the next time an opportunity comes by.

Be a Columbus to whole new continents and worlds within you, opening new channels, not of trade, but of thought.

Henry David Thoreau

Be ready when opportunity comes...Luck is the time when preparation and opportunity meet.

Roy D. Chapin Jr.

Become a possibilitarian. No mater how dark things seem to be or actually are, raise your sights and see possibilities-always see them for they're always there.

Norman Vincent Peale

Before you begin climbing that ladder of success, make sure it's leaning towards the window of opportunity you desire!

Tracy Brinkmann

Chance corrects us of many faults that reason would not know how to correct.

Francois De La Rochefoucauld

Chance favours only those who court her.

Charles Nicolle

Chance generally favours the prudent.

Joseph Joubert

Chance is always powerful. Let your hook be always cast; in the pool where you least expect it, there will be a fish.

Ovid

Chance is the providence of adventurers.

Napoleon Bonaparte

Chance never helps those who do not help themselves.

Sophocles

Jumping at several small opportunities may get us there more quickly than waiting for one big one to come along.

— Hugh Allen

When I look back now over my life and call to mind what I might have had simply for taking and did not take, my heart is like to break.

— William Hale White

Opportunity is often difficult to recognise; we usually expect it to beckon us with beepers and billboards.

— William Arthur Ward

Opportunity is a bird that never perches.

— Claude McDonald

Opportunity is as scarce as oxygen; men fairly breathe it and do not know it.

— Doc Sane

Opportunities do not come with their values stamped upon them.

— Maltbie Babcock

Nothing is so often irretrievably missed as a daily opportunity.

— Marie von Ebner-Eschenbach

It is often hard to distinguish between the hard knocks in life and those of opportunity.

— Frederick Phillips

Seize the opportunity by the beard, for it is bald behind.

— Bulgarian Proverb

I was seldom able to see an opportunity until it had ceased to be one.

— Mark Twain

Ability is of little account without opportunity.

— Napoleon

The secret of success in life is for a man to be ready for his opportunity when it comes.

— Benjamin Disraeli

If opportunity doesn't knock, build a door.

— Milton Berle

Opportunity is a parade. Even as one chance passes, the next is a fife and drum echoing in the distance.

— Robert Brault, www.robertbrault.com

A pessimist is one who makes difficulties of his opportunities and an optimist is one who makes opportunities of his difficulties.

— Harry Truman

Summing up, it is clear the future holds great opportunities. It also holds pitfalls. The trick will be to avoid the pitfalls, seize the opportunities, and get back home by six o'clock.

— Woody Allen, "My Speech to the Graduates,"* Side Effects, *1980

[I]f one wants to get a boat ride, one must be near the river.

***— Anchee Min,* Becoming Madame Mao**

As you seek new opportunity, keep in mind that the sun does not usually reappear on the horizon where last seen.

— Robert Brault, www.robertbrault.com

I held a moment in my hand, brilliant as a star, fragile as a flower, a tiny sliver of one hour. I dripped it carelessly, Ah! I didn't know, I held opportunity.

— Hazel Lee

Every day is an opportunity to make a new happy ending.

— Author Unknown

The follies which a man regrets most in his life are those which he didn't commit when he had the opportunity.

— Helen Rowland

All great work is preparing yourself for the accident to happen.

— Sidney Lumet

When written in Chinese the word "crisis" is composed of two characters—one represents danger and the other represents opportunity.

— John F. Kennedy, address, 12 April 1959

Problems are only opportunities with thorns on them.

— Hugh Miller, **Snow on the Wind**

Opportunity is missed by most people because it is dressed in overalls and looks like work.

— Thomas Edison

Opportunities fly by while we sit regretting the chances we have lost, and the happiness that comes to us we heed not, because of the happiness that is gone.

— Jerome K. Jerome

Grasp your opportunities, no matter how poor your health; *nothing* is worse for your health than boredom.

— Mignon McLaughlin

76

Parenting Quotes

Being a parent is like being pecked to death by a duck. Raising kids is a lot like nailing Jello to a tree. Sometimes, you wonder how can you survive till your kid is grown. Some days, you simply feel grossly inadequate and didn't have clue in the world of what to do next. This series of though-provoking parenting quotes will highlight the ups and downs of being a parent.

A father's goodness is higher than the mountain, a mother's goodness deeper than the sea.

— ***Japanese Proverb***

A person soon learns how little he knows when a child begins to ask questions.

— ***Richard L. Evans***

Affection without sentiment, authority without cruelty, discipline without aggression, humor without ridicule, sacrifice without obligation, companionship without possessiveness.

— ***William E. Blatz***

Affirming words from moms and dads are like light switches. Speak a word of affirmation at the right moment in a child's life and it's like lighting up a whole roomful of possibilities.

— ***Gary Smalley***

Always kiss your children goodnight—even if they're already asleep.

— H. Jackson Brown, Jr.

Before I got married I had six theories about bringing up children; now I have six children, and no theories.

— John Wilmot

Children are the proof we've been here... they are the best thing and the most impossible thing.

— Allison Pearson, I Don't Know How she Does It

Children keep us in check. Their laughter prevents our hearts from hardening. Their dreams ensure we never lose our drive to make ours a better world. They are the greatest disciplinarians known to mankind.

— Queen Rania of Jordan, Hello Magazine

Each day of our lives we make deposits in the memory banks of our children.

— Charles R. Swindoll

Don't demand respect as a parent. Demand civility and insist on honesty. But respect is something you must earn — with kids as well as with adults.

— William Attwood

God sends children to enlarge our hearts, and make us unselfish and full of kindly sympathies and affections.

— Mary Howitt

I just want my kids to love who they are, have happy lives and find something they want to do and make peace with that. Your job as a parent is to give your kids not only the instincts and talents to survive, but help them enjoy their lives.

— Susan Sarandon, Readers' Digest, May 2002

I looked on childrearing not only as a work of love and duty but as a profession that was fully interesting and challenging as any honourable profession in the world and one that demanded the best that I could bring to it.

— Rose Kennedy

If there were no schools to take the children away from home part of the time, the insane asylums would be filled with mothers.

— Edgar W. Howe

If you have never been hated by your child you have never been a parent.

— Bette Davis

If you want children to keep their feet on the ground, put some responsibility on their shoulders.

— Abigail Van Buren

I'm moved by contraries, by opposites, the strength that was my mother's eyes, the beauty of my father's hands.

— Judith Jamison

In spite of the six thousand manuals on child raising in the bookstores, child raising is still a dark continent and no one really knows anything. You just need a lot of love and luck—and, of course, courage.

— Bill Cosby

It kills you to see them grow up. But I guess it would kill you quicker if they didn't.

— Barbara Kingsolver

It's not only children who grow. Parents do too. As much as we watch to see what our children do with their lives, they are watching us to see what we do with ours. I can't tell my children to reach for the sun. All I can do is reach for it, myself.

— Joyce Maynard

Life affords no greater responsibility, no greater privilege, than the raising of the next generation.

— C. Everet Koop, M.D.

Love is the chain whereby to bind a child to its parents.

— Abraham Lincoln

Lucky parents who have fine children usually have lucky children who have fine parents.

— James A. Brewer

Making the decision to have a child is momentous. It is to decide forever to have your heart go walking around outside your body.

— Elizabeth Stone

Many have forgotten this truth, but you must not forget it. You remain responsible, forever, for what you have tamed.

— Antoine De Saint-Exupery

No one knows how children will turn out; a great tree often springs from a tender plant.

— Norwegian proverb

One who walks the road with love will never walk the road alone.

— C. T. Davis

Parents who are afraid to put their foot down usually have children who tread on their toes.

— Chinese Proverb

Parenthood is a lot easier to get into than out of.

— Bruce Lansky

Parenthood: The state of being better chaperoned than you were before marriage.

— Marcelene Cox

Parents can tell but never teach, unless they practice what they preach.

— Arnold Glasow

Parents: People who spend half their time wondering how their children will turn out, and the rest of the time when they will turn in.

— Eleanor Graham Vance

Presence is more than just being there.

— Malcolm Forbes

Raising children is like making biscuits: it is as easy to raise a big batch as one, while you have your hands in the dough.

— E.W. Howe

The best inheritance a parent can give his children is a few minutes of his time each day.

— O. A. Battista

The child supplies the power but the parents have to do the steering.

— Benjamin Spock

The hardest part of raising a child is teaching them to ride bicycles. A shaky child on a bicycle for the first time needs both support and freedom. The realisation that this is what the child will always need can hit hard.

— Sloan Wilson

The Hebrew word for parents is horim, and it comes from the same root as moreh, teacher. The parent is, and remains, the first and most important teacher that the child will have.

— Rabbi Kassel Abelson

The real menance about dealing with a five-year-old is that in no time at all you begin to sound like a five-year-old.

— Jean Kerr

The voice of parents is the voice of gods, for to their children they are heaven's lieutenants.

— Shakespeare

The world talks to the mind. Parents speak more intimately — they talk to the heart.

— Hain Ginott

There are times when parenthood seems nothing but feeding the mouth that bites you.

— Peter de Vries

There are two lasting bequests we can give our children. One is roots. The other is wings.

— Hodding Carter, Jr.

There is no friendship, no love, like that of the parent for the child.

— Henry Ward Beecher

The most important thing that parents can teach their children is how to get along without them.

— Frank A. Clark

To bring up a child in the way he should go, travel that way yourself once in a while.

— Josh Billings

To nourish children and raise them against the odds is, in any time, any place, more valuable than to fix bolts in cars or design nuclear weapons.

— Marilyn French

We may be blinded by our own perceived flaws, but those who love us have clearer vision.

— Sarah Ban Breathnach

We never know the love of our parents for us until we have become parents.

— Henry Ward Beecher

When you have children yourself, you begin to understand what you owe your parents.

— Japanese Proverb

You are the bows from which your children as living arrows are sent forth.

— Kahlil Gibran

You don't really understand human nature unless you know why a child on a merry-go-round will wave at his parents every time around—and why his parents will always wave back.

— William D. Tammeus

You have a lifetime to work, but children are only young once.

— Polish Proverb

77

Passion Quotes

When you have passion for your work, naturally you will be motivated and driven. You are even willing to go the extra mile without much prodding from others. Because you are passionate about doing that thing, and you are following what your heart wants you to do. Let these inspirational passion quotes illustrate the importance of having passion in your life, and being passionate about what you are doing.

A great leader's courage to fulfil his vision comes from passion, not position.

— ***John Maxwell***

A strong passion for any object will ensure success, for the desire of the end will point out the means.

— ***William Hazlitt***

Absence diminishes little passions and increases great ones, as wind extinguishes candles and fans a fire.

— ***François de la Rochefoucauld***

Chase down your passion like it's the last bus of the night.

— ***Glade Byron Addams***

Develop a passion for learning. If you do, you will never cease to grow.

— ***Anthony J. D'Angelo***

Don't ask yourself what the world needs; ask yourself what makes you come alive. And then go and do that. Because what the world needs is people who have come alive.

— Harold Whitman

Follow your passion, and success will follow you.

— Arthur Buddhold

Great dancers are not great because of their technique; they are great because of their passion.

— Martha Graham

If there is no passion in your life, then have you really lived? Find your passion, whatever it may be. Become it, and let it become you and you will find great things happen FOR you, TO you and BECAUSE of you.

— T. Alan Armstrong

If you have ever felt such tremendous enthusiasm and desire for something that you would gladly spend all your waking hours working on it, that you would happily do without pay, then you have found your passion.

— Sharon Cook & Graciela Sholander

It is the soul's duty to be loyal to its own desires. It must abandon itself to its master passion.

— Rebecca West

Making sure our goals are properly aligned with our passions only makes sense.

— Josh Hinds

Never underestimate the power of passion.

— Eve Sawyer

Nothing great in the world has been accomplished without passion.

— Georg Wilhelm Friedrich Hegel

Only passions, great passions, can elevate the soul to great things.

— Denis Diderot

Passion is in all great searches and is necessary to all creative endeavours.

— W. Eugene

Passion that is so deep within that all we need to do is release the passion inside so that we become energised with a newness that all will want to share in.

— M. Lee

So try to pursue the very things that you are passionate about- that is the difference between good and great!

— Shawn Doyle

The greatest gift is a passion for reading. It is cheap, it consoles, it distracts, it excites, it gives you knowledge of the world and experience of a wide kind. It is a moral illumination.

— Elizabeth Hardwick

The more intensely we feel about an idea or a goal, the more assuredly the idea, buried deep in our subconscious, will direct us along the path to its fulfillment.

— Earl Nightingale

The most beautiful make-up of a woman is passion. But cosmetics are easier to buy.

— Yves Saint Laurent

We all need to look into the dark side of our nature— that's where the energy is, the passion. People are afraid of that because it holds pieces of us we're busy denying.

— Sue Grafton

With out passion you don't have energy, with out energy you have nothing.

— Donald Trump

When work, commitment, and pleasure all become one and you reach that deep well where passion lives, nothing is impossible.

— Nancy Coey

78

Persistence Quotes

Persistence quotes points out the one big factor that set the successful people apart from the rest—the quality of being persistent. Of perseverance and never giving up. Enjoy these persistence quotes and may they rekindle your spark to go after your heart's desires.

Being defeated is only a temporary condition; giving up is what makes it permanent.

— ***Marilyn vos Savant***

Between you and every goal that you wish to achieve, there is a series of obstacles, and the bigger the goal, the bigger the obstacles. Your decision to be, have and do something out of the ordinary entails facing difficulties and challenges that are out of the ordinary as well. Sometimes your greatest asset is simply your ability to stay with it longer than anyone else.

— ***Brian Tracy***

Big shots are only little shots who keep shooting.

— ***Christopher Morley***

Courage is being afraid but going on anyhow.

— ***Dan Rather***

Decide carefully, exactly what you want in life, then work like mad to make sure you get it!

— ***Hector Crawford***

Effort is a commitment to seeing a task through to the end, not just until you get tired of it.

— Howard Cate

For now you know one of the greatest principles of success; if you persist long enough you will win.

— Og Mandino

Just don't give up trying to do what you really want to do. Where there's love and inspiration, I don't think you can go wrong.

— Ella Fitzgerald

Keep on going, and the chances are that you will stumble on something, perhaps when you are least expecting it. I never heard of anyone ever stumbling on something sitting down.

— Charles F. Kettering

It does not matter how slowly you go so long as you do not stop.

— Confucius

I don't wait for moods. You accomplish nothing if you do that. Your mind must know it has to get down to work.

— Pearl Buck

I think a hero is an ordinary individual who finds strength to persevere and endure in spite of overwhelming obstacles.

— Christopher Reeve

If one dream should fall and break into a thousand pieces, never be afraid to pick one of those pieces up and begin again.

— Flavia Weedn

If you have made mistakes, there is always another chance for you. You may have a fresh start any moment you choose, for this thing we call 'failure' is not the falling down, but the staying down.

— Mary Pickford

It is by tiny steps that we ascend the stars.

— Jack Leedstrom

It's a funny thing about life; if you refuse to accept anything but the best, you very often get it.

— W. Somerset Maugham

Let me tell you the secret that has led me to my goal: my strength lies solely in my tenacity.

— Louis Pasteur

Many of life's failures are people who did not realise how close they were to success when they gave up.

— Thomas Edison

Most of the important things in the world have been accomplished by people who have kept on trying when there seemed to be no hope at all.

— Dale Carnegie

Never give up on what you love because some one makes fun of you. Never quit or give up. You will make it through.

— Jessie Zaylo

Never, never, never, never give up.

— Winston Churchill

No trumpets sound when the important decisions of our life are made. Destiny is made known silently.

— Agnes De Mille

Nothing in the world can take the place of Persistence. Talent will not; nothing is more common than unsuccessful men with talent. Genius will not; unrewarded genius is almost a proverb. Education will not; the world is full of educated derelicts. Persistence and determination alone are omnipotent. The slogan 'Press On' has solved and always will solve the problems of the human race.

— Calvin Coolidge

Nothing is impossible to a willing heart.

— John Heywood

One has to remember that every failure can be a stepping stone to something better.

— Col. Harland Sanders

Our greatest glory is not in never failing, but in rising up every time we fail.

— Ralph Waldo Emerson

Patience and perseverance have a magical effect before which difficulties disappear and obstacles vanish.

— John Quincy Adams

Perseverance is a great element of success. If you knock long enough and loud enough at the gate, you are sure to wake up somebody.

— Henry Wadsworth Longfellow

Perseverance is failing 19 times and succeeding the 20th.

— Julie Andrews

That which we persist in doing becomes easier, not that the task itself has become easier, but that our ability to perform it has improved.

— Ralph Waldo Emerson

The future belongs to those who believe in the beauty of their dreams.

— Eleanor Roosevelt

The human will, that force unseen, The offspring of a deathless soul,Can hew a wall to any goal, Through walls of granite intervene.

— James Allen

The majority of men meet with failure because of their lack of persistence in creating new plans to take the place of those which fail.

— Napoleon Hill

The person interested in success has to learn to view failure as a healthy, inevitable part of the process of getting to the top.

— Dr. Joyce Brothers

We are made to persist. That's how we find out who we are.

— Tobias Wolff

We can do anything we want as long as we stick to it long enough.

— Helen Keller

When you get into a tight place and everything goes against you, till it seems as though you could not hang on a minute longer, never give up then, for that is just the place and time that the tide will turn.

— Harriet Beecher Stowe

When you get to the end of your rope, tie a knot and hang on.

— Franklin D. Roosevelt

You have to keep plugging away. We are all growing. There is no shortcut. You have to put time into it to build an audience.

— John Gruber

You must keep sending work out; you must never let a manuscript do nothing but eat its head off in a drawer. You send that work out again and again, while you're working on another one. If you have talent, you will receive some measure of success—but only if you persist.

— Isaac Asimov

You will never stub your toe standing still. The faster you go, the more chances there is of stubbing your toe, but the more chance you have of getting somewhere.

— Charles F. Kettering

You're not obligated to win. You're obligated to keep trying to do the best you can every day.

— Marian Wright Edelman

You've got to say, I think that if I keep working at this and want it badly enough I can have it. It's called perseverance.

— Lee Iacocca

79

Pregnancy Quotes

Being pregnant can be one of the most wondrous and magical adventure that you can ever experience. You will most likely feel love, patience and other emotions that bubble up within you. Whether it is your first or fourth, these pregnancy quotes are here to cheer you on being a pregnant woman.

A baby is something you carry inside you for nine months, in your arms for three years and in your heart till the day you die.

— ***Mary Mason***

A grand adventure is about to begin.

— ***Winnie the Pooh***

All the time we wondered and wondered, who is this person coming/growing/turning/floating/swimming deep, deep inside.

— ***Crescent Dragonwagon***

Before you were born I carried you under my heart. From the moment you arrived in this world until the moment I leave it, I will always carry you in my heart.

— ***Mandy Harrison***

Before you were conceived I wanted you
Before you were born I loved you
Before you were here an hour I would die for you
This is the miracle of Mother's Love.

— ***Maureen Hawkins***

Everything grows rounder and wider and weirder, and I sit here in the middle of it all and wonder who in the world you will turn out to be.

— ***Carrie Fisher***

Feeling fat last nine months but the joy of becoming a mom lasts forever.

— ***Nikki Dalton***

I gained 80 pounds for my pregnancy so this is like my coming out party.

— ***Cindy Margolis***

Life is always a rich and steady time when you are waiting for something to happen or to hatch.

— ***E.B. White, Charlotte's Web***

Life is magic, the way nature works seems to be quite magical.

— ***Jonas Salk***

Making a decision to have a child—it's momentous. It is to decide forever to have your heart go walking around outside your body.

— ***Elizabeth Stone***

My family and friends and Rene and the pregnancy fulfilled me with so much love.

— ***Celine Dion***

The most important thing she'd learned over the years was that there was no way to be a perfect mother and a million ways to be a good one.

— ***Jill Churchill***

There are three reasons for breast-feeding: the milk is always at the right temperature; it comes in attractive containers; and the cat can't get it.

— ***Irena Chalmers***

Think of stretch marks as pregnancy service stripes.

— ***Joyce Armor***

80

Present Quotes

Many of us are so busy living in the past or so caught up with planning for tomorrow that we neglect about the most important now, today. These live now quotes will remind you that only now is guaranteed and to live each moment with gusto and zeal. Let these quotes reinforce and bring home the idea that the present moment is to be savored and not live haphazardly.

Children have neither a past nor a future. Thus they enjoy the present – which seldom happens to us.

– ***Jean de la Bruyère***

Don't let the past steal your present.

– ***Cherralea Morgen***

Forever is composed of nows.

– ***Emily Dickinson***

I have realised that the past and future are real illusions, that they exist in the present, which is what there is and all there is.

– ***Alan Watts***

It is only possible to live happily-ever-after on a day-to-day basis.

– ***Margaret Bonnano***

Know the true value of time! Snatch, seize, and enjoy every moment of it. No idleness, no procrastination. Never put off until tomorrow what you can do today.

– ***Philip Chesterfield***

Life is a great and wondrous mystery, and the only thing we know that we have for sure is what is right here right now. Don't miss it.

— Leo Buscaglia

Life is a succession of moments. To live each one is to succeed.

— Coreta Kent

Life lived for tomorrow will always be just a day away from being realised.

— Leo Buscaglia

Living in the moment means letting go of the past and not waiting for the future. It means living your life consciously, aware that each moment you breathe is a gift.

— Oprah Winfrey

Normal day, let me be aware of the treasure you are. Let me learn from you, love you, bless you before you depart. Let me not pass you by in quest of some rare and perfect tomorrow. Let me hold you while I may, for it may not always be so. One day I shall dig my nails into the earth, or bury my face in the pillow, or stretch myself taut, or raise my hands to the sky and want, more than all the world, your return.

— Mary Jean Iron

One of the most tragic things I know about human nature is that all of us tend to put off living. We are all dreaming of some magical rose garden over the horizon—instead of enjoying the roses that are blooming outside our windows today.

— Dale Carnegie

One today is worth two tomorrows.

— Benjamin Franklin

Present-moment living, getting in touch with your "now," is at the heart of effective living. When you think about it, there really is no other moment you can live. Now is all there is, and the future is just another present moment to live when it arrives. One thing is certain, you cannot live it until it does appear.

— Wayne Dyer

Remember then: there is only one time that is important—Now! It is the most important time because it is the only time when we have any power.

— ***Leo Tolstoy***

Stop acting as if life is a rehearsal. Live this day as if it were your last. The past is over and gone. The future is not guaranteed.

— ***Wayne Dyer***

The meeting of two eternities, the past and future....is precisely the present moment.

— ***Henry David Thoreau***

The more I give myself permission to live in the moment and enjoy it without feeling guilty or judgmental about any other time, the better I feel about the quality of my work.

— ***Wayne Dyer***

The other day a man asked me what I thought was the best time of life. "Why," I answered without a thought, "now."

— ***David Grayson***

The past is a guidepost, not a hitching post.

— ***L. Thomas Holdcroft***

There is never time in the future in which we will work out our salvation. The challenge is in the moment; the time is always now.

— ***James Baldwin***

Today is life-the only life you are sure of. Make the most of today. Get interested in something. Shake yourself awake. Develop a hobby. Let the winds of enthusiasm sweep through you. Live today with gusto.

— ***Dale Carnegie***

We are always getting ready to live but never living.

— ***Ralph Waldo Emerson***

We may make our future by the best use of the present. There is no moment like the present.

— ***Maria Edgeworth***

We seem to be going through a period of nostalgia, and everyone seems to think yesterday was better than today. I don't think it was, and I would advise you not to wait ten years before admitting today was great. If you're hung up on nostalgia, pretend today is yesterday and just go out and have one hell of a time.

— *Art Buchwald*

What we are today comes from our thoughts of yesterday, and our present thoughts build our life of tomorrow: Our life is the creation of our mind.

— *Buddha*

When one door closes another door opens; but we so often look so long and so regretfully upon the closed door, that we do not see the ones which open for us.

— *Alexander Graham Bell*

Write down the thoughts of the moment. Those that come unsought for are commonly the most valuable.

— *Francis Bacon*

Yesterday is a canceled check; tomorrow is a promissory note; today is the only cash you have—so spend it wisely.

— *Kay Lyons*

Yesterday is history, tomorrow is a mystery, today is God's gift, that's why we call it the present.

— *Joan Rivers*

You must live in the present, launch yourself on every wave, find your eternity in each moment. Fools stand on their island opportunities and look toward another land. There is no other land, there is no other life but this.

— *Henry David Thoreau*

81

Rabindranath Tagore Quotes

Rabindranath Tagore, the famous Indian poet, novelist, musician, and playwright, educationist reshaped Bengali literature and music in the late 19th and early 20th centuries. As author of *Gitanjali* and its profoundly sensitive, fresh and beautiful verse, he won the 1913 Nobel Prize in Literature. Tagore penned the anthems of Bangladesh and India: *Amar Shonar Bangla* and *Jana Gana Mana*. He is a remarkable man and his wisdom will speak to your heart. Here is a collection of famous quotations by Tagore.

A mind all logic is like a knife all blade. It makes the hand bleed that uses it.

Age considers; youth ventures.

Beauty is truth's smile when she beholds her own face in a perfect mirror.

Bigotry tries to keep truth safe in its hand with a grip that kills it.

Clouds come floating into my life, no longer to carry rain or usher storm, but to add color to my sunset sky.

Death is not extinguishing the light; it is only putting out the lamp because the dawn has come.

Depth of friendship does not depend on length of acquaintance.

Do not say, 'It is morning,' and dismiss it with a name of yesterday. See it for the first time as a newborn child that has no name.

Don't limit a child to your own learning, for he was born in another time.

Emancipation from the bondage of the soil is no freedom for the tree.

Every child comes with the message that God is not yet discouraged of man.

Every difficulty slurred over will be a ghost to disturb your repose later on.

Everything comes to us that belongs to us if we create the capacity to receive it.

Facts are many, but the truth is one.

Faith is the bird that feels the light when the dawn is still dark.

From the solemn gloom of the temple children run out to sit in the dust, God watches them play and forgets the priest.

Gray hairs are signs of wisdom if you hold your tongue, speak and they are but hairs, as in the young.

He who is too busy doing good finds no time to be good.

I have become my own version of an optimist. If I can't make it through one door, I'll go through another door—or I'll make a door. Something terrific will come no matter how dark the present slept and dreamt that life was joy. I awoke and saw that life was service. I acted and behold, service was joy.

If you shut the door to all errors, truth will be shut out.

In Art, man reveals himself and not his objects.

Let us not pray to be sheltered from dangers but to be fearless when facing them.

Let your life lightly dance on the edges of Time like dew on the tip of a leaf.

Life is given to us, we earn it by giving it.

Love does not claim possession, but gives freedom.

Love is an endless mystery, for it has nothing else to explain it.

Love is not a mere impulse, it must contain truth, which is law.

Love is the only reality and it is not a mere sentiment. It is the ultimate truth that lies at the heart of creation.

Music fills the infinite between two souls.

Nirvana is not the blowing out of the candle. It is the extinguishing of the flame because day is come.

The burden of the self is lightened with I laugh at myself.

The butterfly counts not months but moments, and has time enough.

The flower which is single need not envy the thorns that are numerous.

The highest education is that which does not merely give us information but makes our life in harmony with all existence.

The water in a vessel is sparkling; the water in the sea is dark. The small truth has words which are clear; the great truth has great silence.

Those who own much have much to fear.

To be outspoken is easy when you do not wait to speak the complete truth.

Trees are Earth's endless effort to speak to the listening heaven.

82

Religion Quotes

All religions attempt to explain creation, life, and death. These explanations, however diverse, point to God. Get in touch with your soul with these religion quotes. Connect with the supreme being with a clear mind and a pure conscience.

When I do good, I feel good; when I do bad, I feel bad. That's my religion.

– Abraham Lincoln

We have just enough religion to make us hate, but not enough to make us love one another.

– Jonathan Swift

Those who say religion has nothing to do with politics do not know what religion is.

– Mohandas K. Gandhi

Religion is to do right. It is to love, it is to serve, it is to think, it is to be humble.

– Ralph Waldo Emerson

Any religion is forever in danger of petrifaction into mere ritual and habit, though ritual and habit be essential to religion.

– T. S. Eliot

If there were no God, it would have been necessary to invent him.

– Voltaire

True religion is real living; living with all one's soul, with all one's goodness and righteousness.

– Albert Einstein

Lighthouses are more helpful than churches.

– Benjamin Franklin

We can live without religion and meditation, but we cannot survive without human affection.

– Dalai Lama

Doubt is part of all religion. All the religious thinkers were doubters.

– Isaac Bashevis

All religions are founded on the fear of the many and the cleverness of the few.

– Stendhal

Religion consists of a set of things which the average man thinks he believes and wishes he was certain.

– Mark Twain

Religion has caused more harm than any other idea since the beginning of time. There's nothing good I can say about it. People use it as a crutch.

– Larry Flynt

If I had to choose a religion, the sun as the universal giver of life would be my god.

– Napoleon Bonaparte

Just in terms of allocation of time resources, religion is not very efficient. There's a lot more I could be doing on a Sunday morning.

– Bill Gates

You cannot believe in God until you believe in yourself.

– Swami Vivekananda

I love you when you bow in your mosque, kneel in your temple, pray in your church. For you and I are sons of one religion, and it is the spirit.

– Kahlil Gibran

I do not feel obliged to believe that the same God who has endowed us with sense, reason, and intellect has intended us to forgo their use.

– Galileo Galilei

Human beings must be known to be loved; but Divine beings must be loved to be known.

– Blaise Pascal

83

Retirement Quotes

If you are moving into retirement or have already retired, look to these quotes for inspiration and encouragement. Here is a collection of retirement quotes that not only inspire but serve as reminder that there is life after retirement. Besides inspiring retire quotes, there is some quotes that is funny too.

A lot of our friends complain about their retirement. We tell 'emto get a life.

— Larry Laser

A retired husband is often a wife's full-time job.

—Ella Harris

As in all successful ventures, the foundation of a good retirementis planning.

— Earl Nightingale

Don't simply retire from something; have something to retire to.

— Harry Emerson Fosdick

Don't underestimate the value of Doing Nothing, of just going along, listening to all the things you can't hear, and not bothering.

— Pooh's Little Instruction Book, by A.A. Milne

I enjoy waking up and not having to go to work. So I do it three or four times a day.

— Gene Perret

Have you ever been out for a late autumn walk in the closing partof the afternoon, and suddenly looked up to realise that the leaves have practically all gone? And the sun has set and the day gone before you knew it — and with that a cold wind blows across the landscape? That's retirement.

— ***Stephen Leacock***

I'm not just retiring from the company, I'm also retiring from my stress, my commute, my alarm clock, and my iron.

— ***Hartman Jule***

I've been attending lots of seminars in my retirement. They're called naps.

— ***Merri Brownworth***

No longer having to punch a time clock is my definition of retirement. That way I could do what I want — when I want — anytime I want.

— ***Brooky Brown***

Rest is not idleness, and to lie sometimes on the grass under trees on a summer's day, listening to the murmur of the water, or watching the clouds float across the sky, is by no means a waste of time.

— ***J. Lubbock***

Retire from work, but not from life.

— ***M.K. Soni***

Retire? I'm going to stay in show business until I'm the only one left.

— ***George F. Burns***

Retirement has been a discovery of beauty for me. I never had the time before to notice the beauty of my grandkids, my wife, the tree outside my very own front door. And, the beauty of time itself.

— ***Hartman Jule***

Retirement is wonderful. It's doing nothing without worrying about getting caught at it.

— ***Gene Perret***

Retirement itself is the best gift. No gold watch could ever top it.

— Abigail Charleson

Retirement means doing whatever I want to do. It means choice.

— Dianne Nahirny

Sooner or later I'm going to die, but I'm not going to retire.

— Margaret Mead

The trouble with retirement is that you never get a day off.

— Abe Lemons

There are so many other interesting ways to spend your time. I feellike early retirement is a gift, but it's such an incredible gift. It's a gift I need to use.

— Martha Felt-Bardon

There is a whole new kind of life ahead, full of experiences just waiting to happen. Some call it "retirement." I call it bliss.

— Betty Sullivan

We have no porch, no rocking chair— and no time. My biggest need is a calendar because there are so many things to do. Now I encourage people to retire—the younger the better.

— Maurice Musholt

When a man retires, his wife gets twice the husband but only half the income.

— Chi Chi Rodriguez

When men reach their sixties and retire, they go to pieces. Women go right on cooking.

— Gail Sheehy

84

Shakespeare Quotes

William Shakespeare is often called "The Bard" or England's national poet. He is even regarded by some as the greatest writer in the English language. A famous English poet and playwright, his plays have transcended the ages and are still widely studied and performed throughout the world today. Here is a wonderful collection of Shakespeare quotes.

A smile re-cures the wounding of a frown.

— *Venus & Adonis*

All that glisters is not gold.

— *The Merchant of Venice*

All that lives must die, passing through nature to eternity.

— *Hamlet*

All the world's a stage,
And all the men and women merely players;
They have their exits and their entrances,
And one man in his time plays many parts,
His acts being seven ages.

— *As You Like It*

Be not afraid of greatness: some are born great, some achieve greatness, and some have greatness thrust upon 'em.

— *Twelfth Night*

Courage and comfort, all shall yet go well.

— King John

Cowards die many times before their deaths,
The valiant never taste of death but once.

— Julius Caesar

Did my heart love till now? forswear it, sight! For I ne'er saw true beauty till this night.

— Romeo & Juliet

God send everyone their heart's desire!

— Much Ado

Have patience, and endure.

— Much Ado

I am not of that feather, to shake off my friend when he must need me.

— Timon of Athens

I can no other answer make, but, thanks, and thanks.

— Twelfth Night

Its not enough to speak, but to speak true.

— A Midsummer's Night Dream

Kindness, nobler ever than revenge.

— As You Like It

Let me not to the marriage of true minds
Admit impediments. Love is not love
Which alters when it alteration finds,
Or bends with the remover to remove.
O no, it is an ever-fixèd mark
That looks on tempests and is never shaken;
It is the star to every wand'ring bark,
Whose worth's unknown, although his height be taken.

— Sonnet 116

Love all, trust a few, do wrong to none.

— All's Well

Love comforteth like sunshine after rain.

— Venus & Adonis

Love looks not with the eyes but with the mind.

— A Midsummer Night's Dream

Men at some time are masters of their fate.

— Julius Caesar

Neither a borrower nor a lender be,
For loan oft loses both itself and friend,
And borrowing dulls the edge of husbandry.

— Hamlet

Never shame to hear what you have nobly done.

— Coriolanus

Our doubts are traitors, and make us lose the good we oft might win, by fearing to attempt.

— Measure for Measure

Our remedies oft in ourselves do lie,
Which we ascribe to Heaven.

— All's Well That Ends Well

Pray now, forget and forgive.

— King Lear

The course of true love never did run smooth.

— A Midsummer Night's Dream

Therefore, since brevity is the soul of wit.

— Hamlet

Therein the patient
Must minister to himself.

— Macbeth

To be, or not to be, that is the question.

— William Hamlet

Why then 'tis none to you; for there is nothing either good or bad, but thinking makes it so.

— Hamlet

Wisely and slow; they stumble who run fast.

— Romeo & Juliet

85

Sister Quotes

Here is a wonderful collection of sister quotes that illustrate undeniably one of the most meaningful relationships that women can form with another being. Let these quotes about sisters help you out in expressing your millions of incredible feelings towards your younger sisters and older sisters.

Go on, enjoy the list of sister quotes I've collected.

A ministering angel shall my sister be.

— ***William Shakespeare***

A sibling may be the keeper of one's identity, the only person with the keys to one's unfettered, more fundamental self.

— ***Marian Sandmaier***

A sister can be seen as someone who is both ourselves and very much not ourselves—a special kind of double.

— ***Toni Morrison***

A sister is a gift to the heart, a friend to the spirit, a golden thread to the meaning of life.

— ***Isadora James***

A sister is a little bit of childhood that can never be lost.

— ***Marion C. Garretty***

A sister smiles when one tells one's stories—for she knows where the decoration has been added.

— ***Chris Montaigne***

A younger sister is someone to use as a guinea-pig in trying sledges and experimental go-carts. Someone to send on messages to Mum. But someone who needs you—who comes to you with bumped heads, grazed knees, tales of persecution. Someone who trusts you to defend her. Someone who thinks you know the answers to almost everything.

— ***Pam Brown***

An older sister is a friend and defender—a listener, conspirator, a counsellor and a sharer of delights. And sorrows too.

— ***Pam Brown***

Between sisters, often, the child's cry never dies down. "Never leave me," it says; "do not abandon me."

— ***Louise Bernikow***

Big sisters are the crab grass in the lawn of life.

— ***Charles M. Schulz***

Bless you, my darling, and remember you are always in the heart—oh tucked so close there is no chance of escape—of your sister.

— ***Katherine Mansfield***

Elder sisters never can do younger ones justice!

— ***Charlotte M. Yonge***

Having a sister is like having a best friend you can't get rid of. You know whatever you do, they'll still be there.

— ***Amy Li***

Help one another, is part of the religion of sisterhood.

— ***Louisa May Alcott***

How do people make it through life without a sister?

— ***Sara Corpening***

Husbands come and go; children come and eventually they go. Friends grow up and move away. But the one thing that's never lost is your sister.

— ***Gail Sheeny***

I know some sisters who only see each other on Mother's Day and some who will never speak again.

But most are like my sister and me... linked by volatile love, best friends who make other best friends ever so slightly less best.

— Patricia Volk

I would like more sisters, that the taking out of one, might not leave such stillness.

— Emily Dickinson

If sisters were free to express how they really feel, parents would hear this: "Give me all the attention and all the toys and send Rebecca to live with Grandma."

— Linda Sunshine

If we believed in the media we would think the only significant relationship in our lives is a romantic one. Yet sisterhood is probably the one that will last longer than any other... a sister will always be around.

— Jane Dowdeswell

If you don't understand how a woman could both love her sister dearly and want to wring her neck at the same time, then you were probably an only child.

— Linda Sunshine

If your sister is in a tearing hurry to go out and cannot catch your eye, she's wearing your best sweater.

— Pam Brown

In thee my soul shall own combined the sister and the friend.

— Catherine Killigrew

Is solace anywhere more comforting than in the arms of a sister.

— Alice Walker

It's hard to be responsible, adult and sensible all the time. How good it is to have a sister whose heart is as young as your own.

— Pam Brown

More than Santa Claus, your sister knows when you've been bad and good.

— Linda Sunshine

My sister taught me everything I really need to know, and she was only in sixth grade at the time.

— ***Linda Sunshine***

Of two sisters one is always the watcher, one the dancer.

— ***Louise Glück***

One of the best things about being an adult is the realisation that you can share with your sister and still have plenty for yourself.

— ***Betsy Cohen***

Our brothers and sisters are there with us from the dawn of our personal stories to the inevitable dusk.

— ***Susan Scarf Merrell***

Our siblings push buttons that cast us in roles we felt sure we had let go of long ago—the baby, the peacekeeper, the caretaker, the avoider.... It doesn't seem to matter how much time has elapsed or how far we've travelled.

— ***Jane Mersky Leder***

Our siblings. They resemble us just enough to make all their differences confusing, and no matter what we choose to make of this, we are cast in relation to them our whole lives long.

— ***Susan Scarf Merrell***

She is your mirror, shining back at you with a world of possibilities. She is your witness, who sees you at your worst and best, and loves you anyway. She is your partner in crime, your midnight companion, someone who knows when you are smiling, even in the dark. She is your teacher, your defense attorney, your personal press agent, even your shrink. Some days, she's the reason you wish you were an only child.

— ***Barbara Alpert***

Siblings are the people we practice on, the people who teach us about fairness and cooperation and kindness and caring—quite often the hard way.

— ***Pamela Dugdale***

Sisterhood is powerful.

— ***Robin Morgan***

Sisterly love is, of all sentiments, the most abstract. Nature does not grant it any functions.

— Ugo Betti

Sisters annoy, interfere, criticise. Indulge in monumental sulks, in huffs, in snide remarks. Borrow. Break. Monopolise the bathroom. Are always underfoot. But if catastrophe should strike, sisters are there. Defending you against all comers.

— Pam Brown

Sisters don't need words. They have perfected a language of snarls and smiles and frowns and winks—expressions of shocked surprise and incredulity and disbelief. Sniffs and snorts and gasps and sighs—that can undermine any tale you're telling.

— Pam Brown

Sisters function as safety nets in a chaotic world simply by being there for each other.

— Carol Saline

Sisters share the scent and smells—the feel of a common childhood.

— Pam Brown

Sisters is probably the most competitive relationship within the family, but once the sisters are grown, it becomes the strongest relationship.

— Margaret Mead

Sisters never quite forgive each other for what happened when they were five.

— Pam Brown

Sweet is the voice of a sister in the season of sorrow.

— Benjamin Disraeli

The best thing about having a sister was that I always had a friend.

— Cali Rae Turner

The mildest, drowsiest sister has been known to turn tiger if her sibling is in trouble.

— Clara Ortega

There can be no situation in life in which the conversation of my dear sister will not administer some comfort to me.

— Mary Montagu

To the outside world we all grow old. But not to brothers and sisters. We know each other as we always were. We know each other's hearts. We share private family jokes. We remember family feuds and secrets, family griefs and joys. We live outside the touch of time.

— Clara Ortega

We acquire friends and we make enemies, but our sisters come with the territory.

— Evelyn Loeb

We know one another's faults, virtues, catastrophes, mortifications, triumphs, rivalries, desires, and how long we can each hang by our hands to a bar. We have been banded together under pack codes and tribal laws.

— Rose Macaulay

We may look old and wise to the outside world. But to each other, we are still in junior school.

— Charlotte Gray

Whatever you do they will love you; even if they don't love you they are connected to you till you die. You can be boring and tedious with sisters, whereas you have to put on a good face with friends.

— Deborah Moggach

What's the good of news if you haven't a sister to share it?

— Jenny DeVries

When sisters stand shoulder to shoulder, who stands a chance against us?

— Pam Brown

You can kid the world. But not your sister.

— Charlotte Gray

You keep your past by having sisters. As you get older, they're the only ones who don't get bored if you talk about your memories.

— Deborah Moggach

86

Smile and Laughter Quotes

Laughter, some said it is the best medicine in the world. So start smiling and laughing as much as you can. Have a hearty laugh over every amusing situation. Laugh even at yourself and smile at the simplest pleasures in your life. With smiles and laughter, your days will become lighter, more joyous and more bearable even on those hay-wired days. Your smiling face looks much more appealing and beautiful too. Threse smile and laughter quotes will show how smiles and laughter can make your days sparkle with happiness.

A good laugh and a long sleep are the best cures in the doctor's book.

— ***Irish Proverb***

A hearty laugh gives one a dry cleaning, while a good cry is a wet wash.

— ***Puzant Kevork Thomajan***

A kind heart is a fountain of gladness, making everything in its vicinity freshen into smiles.

— ***Washington Irving***

A laugh is a smile that bursts.

— ***Mary H. Waldrip***

A man isn't poor if he can still laugh.

— ***Raymond Hitchcock***

A smile appeared upon her face as if she'd taken it directly from her handbag and pinned it there.

— Loma Chandler

A smile is a curve that sets everything straight.

— Phyllis Diller

A smile is an inexpensive way to change your looks.

— Charles Gordy

A smile is the universal welcome.

— Max Eastman

All the statistics in the world can't measure the warmth of a smile.

— Chris Hart

At the height of laughter, the universe is flung into a kaleidoscope of new possibilities.

— Jean Houston

Beauty is power; a smile is its sword.

— Charles Reade

Before you put on a frown, make absolutely sure there are no smiles available.

— Jim Beggs

Carry laughter with you wherever you go.

— Hugh Sidey

Everytime you smile at someone, it is an action of love, a gift to that person, a beautiful thing.

— Mother Teresa

I am thankful for laughter, except when milk comes out of my nose.

— Woody Allen

I live by this credo: Have a little laugh at life and look around you for happiness instead of sadness. Laughter has always brought me out of unhappy situations. Even in your darkest moment, you usually can find something to laugh about if you try hard enough.

— Red Skelton

If you smile when no one else is around, you really mean it.

— Andy Rooney

It is impossible for you to be angry and laugh at the same time. Anger and laughter are mutually exclusive and you have the poser to choose either.

— ***Wayne Dyer***

Laugh at yourself, but don't ever aim your doubt at yourself. Be bold. When you embark for strange places, don't leave any of yourself safely on shore. Have the nerve to go into unexplored territory.

— ***Alan Alda***

Laughter and tears are both responses to frustration and exhaustion. I myself prefer to laugh, since there is less cleaning up to do afterward.

— ***Kurt Vonnegut***

Laughter gives us distance. It allows us to step back from an event, deal with it and then move on.

— ***Bob Newhart***

Laughter is a tranquiliser with no side effects.

— ***Arnold Glasow***

Laughter is an instant vacation.

— ***Milton Berle***

Laughter is the corrective force which prevents us from becoming cranks.

— ***Henri Bergson***

Laughter is the sensation of feeling good all over and showing it principally in one place.

— ***Josh Billings***

Laughter is the shortest distance between two people.

— ***Victor Borge***

Laughter is the sun that drives winter from the human face.

— ***Victor Hugo***

Laughter on one's lips is a sign that the person down deep has a pretty good grasp of life.

— ***Hugh Sidey***

I've always thought that a big laugh is a really loud noise from the soul saying, "Ain't that the truth."

— ***Quincy Jones***

Man, when you lose your laugh you lose your footing.

— Ken Kesey

Mirth is God's medicine. Everybody ought to bathe in it.

— Henry Ward Beecher

Nothing shows a man's character more than what he laughs at.

— Johann Wolfgang von Goethe

Of all the things you wear, your expression is the most important.

— Janet Lane

Peace begins with a smile.

— Mother Teresa

People seldom notice old clothes if you wear a big smile.

— Lee Mildon

Perhaps I know best why it is man alone who laughs; he alone suffers so deeply that he had to invent laughter.

— Friedrich Nietzsche

Really, sex and laughter do go very well together, and I wondered—and I still do—which is more important.

— Hermione Gingold

Remember, men need laughter sometimes more than food.

— Anna Fellows Johnston

She gave me a smile I could feel in my hip pocket.

— Raymond Chandler

Smile. Have you ever noticed how easily puppies make human friends? Yet all they do is wag their tails and fall over.

— Walter Anderson

So many tangles in life are ultimately hopeless that we have no appropriate sword other than laughter.

— Gordon W. Allport

Seven days without laughter makes one weak.

— Mort Walker

Start every day with a smile and get it over with.

— W.C. Fields

That is the best—to laugh with someone because you both think the same things are funny.

— Gloria Vanderbilt

The human race has only one really effective weapon and that is laughter.

— Mark Twain

The most wasted of all days is one without laughter.

— E.E. Cummings

The person who knows how to laugh at himself will never cease to be amused.

— Shirley MacLaine

There can never be enough said of the virtues, dangers, the power of a shared laugh.

— Françoise Sagan

Wear a smile and have friends; wear a scowl and have wrinkles.

— George Eliot

What soap is to the body, laughter is to the soul.

— Yiddish Proverb

With the fearful strain that is on me night and day, if I did not laugh I should die.

— Abraham Lincoln

Wrinkles should merely indicate where smiles have been.

— Mark Twain

You can't deny laughter; when it comes, it plops down in your favorite chair and stays as long as it wants.

— Stephen King

You're never fully dressed without a smile.

— Martin Charnin

87

Socrates Quotes

Socrates is synonymous with philosophy. One of the earliest known philosophers, Socrates laid the foundation for Western philosophy. Unfortunately, Socrates did not publish his philosophy. So most of the information about Socrates is gathered from Plato's writings. You will discover gems of wisdom in these quotes of Socrates, the enigmatic philosopher.

Be as you wish to seem.

Employ your time in improving yourself by other men's writings so that you shall come easily by what others have laboured hard for.

He is the richest who is content with the least.

Let him who would move the world first move himself.

Nothing can harm a good man, either in life or after death.

The nearest way to glory is to strive to be what you wish to be thought to be.

The unexamined life is not worth living.

As for me, all I know is that I know nothing.

Be as you wish to seem.

I know that I am intelligent, because I know that I know nothing.

Let him that would move the world first move himself.

Not life, but good life, is to be chiefly valued.

Wisdom begins in wonder.

By all means marry; if you get a good wife, you'll be happy. If you get a bad one, you'll become a philosopher.

Do not do to others what angers you if done to you by others.

If a man is proud of his wealth, he should not be praised until it is known how he employs it.

Remember what is unbecoming to do is also unbecoming to speak of.

The only good is knowledge and the only evil is ignorance.

Thou shouldst eat to live; not live to eat.

88

Self-development Quotes

Whether you have always been on the journey of developing yourself, or you have just started, these quotes will inspire, motivate and encourage you on this wondrous journey of self-discovery and self-improvement. Here is an inspiring series of self-development quotes to cheer you on, as you strive to improve yourself each and every day.

A man's mind stretched by a new idea can never go back to its original dimensions.

— Oliver Wendell Holmes

Be a student. Stay open and willing to learn from everyone and anyone. Being a student means you have room for new input. When you are green you grow, when you are ripe you rot. By staying green you will avoid the curse of being an expert. When you know in your heart that every single person you encounter in your lifetime has something to teach you, you are able to utilise their offerings in a profound way.

— Dr Wayne W Dyer

Change and growth take place when a person has risked himself and dares to become involved with experimenting with his own life.

— Herbert Otto

Knowing yourself is the beginning of all wisdom.

— Aristotle

Everybody wants to be somebody; nobody wants to grow.

– Johann Wolfgang von Goethe

Everything we would ever need to become rich and powerful and sophisticated is within our reach. The major reason that so few take advantage of all that we have is simply, neglect.

– Jim Rohn

Exert your talents, and distinguish yourself, and don't think of retiring from the world, until the world will be sorry that you retire.

– Samuel Johnson

He who would govern others, first should be master of himself.

– Philip Massinger

I am always doing that which I can not do, in order that I may learn how to do it.

– Pablo Picasso

If you deliberately plan on being less than you are capable of being, then I warn you that you'll be unhappy for the rest of your life.

– Abraham H Maslow

If you want more, you have to require more from yourself.

– Dr Phil

I'm convinced that we can write and live our own scripts more than most people will acknowledge. I also know the price that must be paid. It's a real struggle to do it. It requires visualisation and affirmation. It involves living a life of integrity, starting with making and keeping promises, until the whole human personality the senses, the thinking, the feeling, and the intuition are ultimately integrated and harmonised.

– Stephen Covey

It doesn't matter who you are, where you come from. The ability to triumph begins with you. Always.

– Oprah Winfrey

Most people never feel secure because they are always worried that they will lose their job, lose the money they already have, lose their spouse, lose their health, and so on. The only true security in life comes from knowing that every single day you are improving yourself in some way, that you are increasing the caliber of who you are and that you are valuable to your company, your friends, and your family.

— ***Anthony Robbins***

Most people struggle with life balance simply because they haven't paid the price to decide what is really important to them.

— ***Stephen Covey***

Never again clutter your days or nights with so many menial and unimportant things that you have no time to accept a real challenge when it comes along. This applies to play as well as work. A day merely survived is no cause for celebration. You are not here to fritter away your precious hours when you have the ability to accomplish so much by making a slight change in your routine. No more busy work. No more hiding from success. Leave time, leave space, to grow. Now. Now! Not tomorrow!

— ***Og Mandino***

Of all the things that can have an effect on your future, I believe personal growth is the greatest. We can talk about sales growth, profit growth, asset growth, but all of this probably will not happen without personal growth.

— ***Jim Rohn***

One of the marks of excellent people is that they never compare themselves with others. They only compare themselves with themselves and with their past accomplishments and future potential.

— ***Brian Tracy***

Our ideas, like orange-plants, spread out in proportion to the size of the box which imprisons the roots.

— ***Edward Bulwer Lytton***

The aim of life is self-development. To realise one's nature perfectly—that is what each of us is here for.

— ***Oscar Wilde***

The highest reward for a person's toil is not what they get for it, but what they become by it.

— ***John Ruskin***

The process of self-development can be described as the stripping away of layer after layer of all that is false.

— ***The Daily Guru***

The well bred contradict other people. The wise contradict themselves.

— ***Oscar Wilde***

There is only one corner of the universe you can be certain of improving, and that's your own self.

—***Aldous Huxley***

When it comes right down to it, all you have is your self. Your Self is a sun with a thousand rays...

— ***Pablo Picasso***

When I let go of what I am, I become what I might be.

— ***John Heider***

You seek too much information and not enough transformation.

— ***Sai Baba***

89

Sports Quotes

A winning collection of sports quotes to motivate and inspire. If you are looking for quotes about sports, don't miss this series.Besides physical training and preparation, one has to go through plenty of positive and inspirational mental training to push one to excel in sports. Use these sports quotations to encourage yourself, your family members or friends in their sports training and competitions.

Adversity cause some men to break; others to break records.

— ***William A. Ward***

Champions aren't made in the gyms. Champions are made from something they have deep inside them — a desire, a dream, a vision.

— ***Muhammad Ali***

Champions keep playing until they get it right.

— ***Billie Jean King***

Competing in sports has taught me that if I'm not willing to give 120 percent, somebody else will.

— ***Ron Blomberg***

Develop the winning edge; small differences in your performance can lead to large differences in your results.

— ***Brian Tracy***

Don't look back. Something might be gaining on you.

— Satchel Paige

Every day, in every way, I am getting better and better.

— Emile Coue

Even if you are on the right track, you'll get run over if you just sit there.

— Will Rogers

Face each day with the expectation of achieving good, rather than the dread of falling short.

— Shannon Miller

How you respond to the challenge in the second half will determine what you become after the game, whether you are a winner or a loser.

— Lou Holtz

I learned that if you want to make it bad enough, no matter how bad it is, you can make it.

— Gale Sayers

I think self-awareness is probably the most important thing towards being a champion.

— Billie Jean King

If at first you don't succeed, you are running about average.

— M.H. Alderson

If you train hard, you'll not only be hard, you'll be hard to beat.

— Herschel Walker

In order to excel, you must be completely dedicated to your chosen sport. You must also be prepared to work hard and be willing to accept destructive criticism. Without 100% dedication, you won't be able to do this.

— Wilson Mizner

In sports, you simply aren't considered a real champion until you have defended your title successfully. Winning it once can be a fluke; winning it twice proves you are the best.

— Althea Gibson

It is a rough road that leads to the heights of greatness.

— Seneca

It's a little like wrestling a gorilla. You don't quit when you're tired you quit when the gorilla is tired.

— Robert Strauss

It's never been easy. But I've always wanted to play hockey. I love hockey. I'd rather play hockey than do anything else. If you have that kind of desire, I think you can achieve what you want to achieve.

— Manon Rheaume

I've always made a total effort, even when the odds seemed entirely against me. I never quit trying; I never felt that I didn't have a chance to win.

— Arnold Palmer

I've missed more than 9000 shots in my career. I've lost almost 300 games. 26 times, I've been trusted to take the game winning shot and missed. I've failed over and over and over again in my life. And that is why I succeed.

— Michael Jordan

Live daringly, boldly, fearlessly. Taste the relish to be found in competition—in having put forth the best within you.

— Henry J. Kaiser

My motto was always to keep swinging. Whether I was in a slump or feeling badly or having trouble off the field, the only thing to do was keep swinging.

— Hank Aaron

Mind is everything: muscle—pieces of rubber. All that I am, I am because of my mind.

— Paavo Nurmi

No matter how tough, no matter what kind of outside pressure, no matter how many bad breaks along the way, I must keep my sights on the final goal, to win, win, win—and with more love and passion than the world has ever witnessed in any performance.

—Billie Jean King

No steam or gas drives anything until it is confined. No life ever grows great until it is focused, dedicated, disciplined.

— ***Harry Emerson Fosdick D. D***

Obstacles are those frightful things you see when you take your eyes off your goals.

— ***Sydney Smith***

One of the things that my parents have taught me is never listen to other people's expectations. You should live your own life and live up to your own expectations, and those are the only things I really care about it.

— ***Tiger Woods***

Pain is temporary. It may last a minute, or an hour, or a day, or a year, but eventually it will subside and something else will take its place. If I quit, however, it lasts forever.

— ***Lance Armstrong***

Regardless of how you feel inside, always try to look like a winner. Even if you are behind, a sustained look of control and confidence can give you a mental edge that results in victory.

— ***Arthur Ashe***

Show me a guy who's afraid to look bad, and I'll show you a guy you can beat every time.

— ***Lou Brock***

The best and fastest way to learn a sport is to watch and imitate a champion.

— ***Jean-Claude Killy***

The most powerful weapon on earth is the human soul on fire.

— ***Ferdinand Foch***

The will to win is important, but the will to prepare is vital.

— ***Joe Paterno***

The winners in life think constantly in terms of I can, I will, and I am. Losers, on the other hand, concentrate their waking thoughts on what they should have or would have done, or what they can't do.

— ***Dennis Waitley***

There are only two options regarding commitment. You're either IN or you're OUT. There is no such thing as life in-between.

— ***Pat Riley***

To succeed...You need to find something to hold on to, something to motivate you, something to inspire you.

— ***Tony Dorsett***

We are what we repeatedly do. Excellence, therefore, is not an act but a habit.

— ***Aristotle***

When someone tells me there is only one way to do things, it always lights a fire under my butt. My instant reaction is, 'I'm gonna prove you wrong.'

— ***Picabo Street***

When you're riding, only the race in which you're riding is important.

— ***Bill Shoemaker***

Yesterday I dared to struggle. Today I dare to win.

— ***Bernadette Devlin***

You can become a winner only if you are willing to walk over the edge.

— ***Damon Runyon***

You can't put a limit on anything. The more you dream, the farther you get.

— ***Michael Phelps***

You have to learn the rules of the game. And then you have to play better than anyone else.

— ***Albert Einstein***

You miss 100% of the shots you never take.

— ***Wayne Gretzky***

90

Strength Quotes

Life can be filled with challenges. Sometimes you just feel totally beaten up and need comforting arms and encouraging thoughts to soothe your soul. Look within yourself to find your strength. We gain strength through practice and making efforts to learn from mistakes. Here is a beautiful series of strength quotes to keep you going on when you feel that you have reached the end of your wits.

A hero is an ordinary individual who finds the strength to persevere and endure in spite of overwhelming obstacles.

— ***Christopher Reeve***

Anyone can give up, it's the easiest thing in the world to do. But to hold it together when everyone else would understand if you fell apart, that's true strength.

— ***Author Unknown***

Confront the dark parts of yourself, and work to banish them with illumination and forgiveness. Your willingness to wrestle with your demons will cause your angels to sing. Use the pain as fuel, as a reminder of your strength.

— ***August Wilson***

Go within every day and find the inner strength so that the world will not blow your candle out.

— ***Katherine Dunham***

If your heart acquires strength, you will be able to remove blemishes from others without thinking evil of them.

— Mahatma Gandhi

It does not take much strength to do things, but it requires great strength to decide on what to do.

— Elbert Hubbard

It takes more courage to reveal insecurities than to hide them, more strength to relate to people than to dominate them, more 'manhood' to abide by thought-out principles rather than blind reflex. Toughness is in the soul and spirit, not in muscles and an immature mind.

— Alex Karras

It is time for parents to teach young people early on that in diversity there is beauty and there is strength.

— Maya Angelou

Knowing others is intelligence; knowing yourself is true wisdom. Mastering others is strength; mastering yourself is true power. If you realise that you have enough, you are truly rich.

— Tao Te Ching

Life is very interesting... in the end, some of your greatest pains, become your greatest strengths.

— Drew Barrymore

Our strength grows out of our weaknesses.

— Ralph Waldo Emerson

Strength does not come from physical capacity. It comes from an indomitable will.

— Mahatma Gandhi

Strength does not come from winning. Your struggles develop your strengths. When you go through hardships and decide not to surrender, that is strength.

— Arnold Schwarzenegger

Strength is a matter of the made-up mind.

— John Beecher

The size of your success is measured by the strength of your desire; the size of your dream; and how you handle disappointment along the way.

— Robert Kiyosaki

Those who contemplate the beauty of the earth find reserves of strength that will endure as long as life lasts.

— Rachel Carson

We acquire the strength we have overcome.

— Ralph Waldo Emerson

We gain strength, and courage, and confidence by each experience in which we really stop to look fear in the face... we must do that which we think we cannot.

— Eleanor Roosevelt

When I dare to be powerful—to use my strength in the service of my vision, then it becomes less and less important whether I am afraid.

— Audre Lorde

When you get to the end of your rope, tie a knot and hang on.

— Franklin D. Roosevelt

Women are like teabags. We don't know our true strength until we are in hot water!

— Eleanor Roosevelt

91

Success Quotes

Success means different things to different people. To some, success is purely in monetary-term and becoming a millionaire is the number one goal. Success could also mean achieving fame or title by becoming a singing sensation or CEO of some public-listed company. To others, success simply means giving one's best shot in whatever one's doing. Whatever success means to you, if you think it is worthwhile, it's worth pursuing. Get inspired by these success quotes and may you be encouraged by these quotes.

> Cherish your visions and your dreams, as they are the children of your soul, the blueprints of your ultimate achievements.
>
> — ***Napoleon Hill***

> For true success ask yourself these four questions: Why? Why not? Why not me? Why not now?
>
> — ***James Allen***

> If one advances confidently in the direction of one's dreams, and endeavors to live the life which one has imagined, one will meet with a success unexpected in common hours.
>
> — ***Henry David Thoreau***

> No man ever achieved worth-while success who did not, at one time or other, find himself with at least one foot hanging well over the brink of failure.
>
> — ***Napoleon Hill***

Only those who will risk going too far can possibly find out how far one can go.

– T.S. Eliot

Picture yourself vividly as winning, and that alone will contribute immeasurably to your success.

– Harry Emerson Fosdick

Success is a state of mind. If you want success, start thinking of yourself as a success.

– Dr. Joyce Brothers

Success is going from failure to failure without losing enthusiasm.

– Winston Churchill

Success is not to be pursued; it is to be attracted by the person you become.

– Jim Rohn

Success means having the courage, the determination, and the will to become the person you believe you were meant to be.

– George Sheehan

Success seems to be connected with action. Successful people keep moving. They make mistakes, but they don't quit.

– Conrad Hilton

Take up one idea. Make that one idea your life—think of it, dream of it, live on idea. Let the brain, muscles, nerves, every part of your body, be full of that idea, and just leave every other idea alone. This is the way to success.

– Swami Vivekananda

The best place to succeed is where you are with what you have.

– Charles Schwab

The door to a balanced success opens widest on the hinges of hope and encouragement.

– Zig Ziglar

The person interested in success has to learn to view failure as a healthy, inevitable part of the process of getting to the top.

— Dr. Joyce Brothers

To laugh often and much; to win the respect of intelligent people; to appreciate beauty; to find the best in others; to leave the world a bit better, whether by a healthy child, a garden patch, or a redeemed social condition; to know even one life has breathed easier because you have lived. This is to have succeeded!

— Ralph Waldo Emerson

To succeed in life, we must dream the dream of imaginational achievement.

—Samuel Adinoyi

Vision is not enough; it must be combined with venture. It is not enough to stare up the steps. We must step up the stairs.

— Vaclav Havel

Welcome every morning with a smile. Look on the new day as another special gift from your Creator, another golden opportunity to complete what you were unable to finish yesterday. Be a self-starter. Let your first hour set the theme of success and positive action that is certain to echo through your entire day. Today will never happen again. Don't waste it with a false start or no start at all. You were not born to fail.

— Og Mandino

When we see problems as opportunities for growth, we tap a source of knowledge within ourselves which carries us through.

— Marsha Sinetar

Whenever you see a successful business, someone once made a courageous decision.

— Peter Drucker

Whether you think you can or think you can't—you are right.

— Henry Ford

92

Summer Quotes

Summer is definitely a strong and commanding season, where it leaves many traces of its presence. After being trapped with indoor activities for months, now it's the time to break free and bask in the warm sunshine! There's a burst of activities everywhere. Kids swimming in the rivers, beaches and swimming pools. Adults fishing, reading, and picnicking. Enjoy the sunshine while it last and have fun with these summer quotes.

A life without love is like a year without summer.

— ***Swedish Proverb***

A perfect summer day is when the sun is shining, the breeze is blowing, the birds are singing, and the lawn mower is broken.

— ***James Dent***

A single sunbeam is enough to drive away many shadows.

— ***St. Francis of Assisi***

Ah, summer, what power you have to make us suffer and like it.

— ***Russel Baker***

August creates as she slumbers, replete and satisfied.

— ***Joseph Wood Krutch***

Be intent upon the perfection of the present day.

— William Law

Be like the flower, turn your face to the sun.

— Kahlil Gibran

Being a child at home alone in the summer is a high-risk occupation. If you call your mother at work thirteen times an hour, she can hurt you.

— Erma Bombeck

Breathless, we flung us on a windy hill, laughed in the sun, and kissed the lovely grass.

— Rupert Brooke

Celebrate Summer—Sun drenched days and starlit nights...

— Gooseberry Patch

Colored scents that fill the air as drowsy insects hum around in the meadow is the place of secret magic where nature alone renews itself.

— Kate Bergquist

Deep summer is when laziness finds respectability.

— Sam Keen

Dirty hands, iced tea, garden fragrances thick in the air and a blanket of color before me, who could ask for more?

— Bev Adams

Heat, ma'am! it was so dreadful here, that I found there was nothing left for it but to take off my flesh and sit in my bones.

— Sydney Smith

I know that if odour were visible, as colour is, I'd see the summer garden in rainbow clouds.

— Robert Bridges

I question not if thrushes sing,
If roses load the air;
Beyond my heart I need not reach
When all is summer there.

— John Vance Cheney

I wonder what it would be like to live in a world where it was always June.

— L. M. Montgomery

If a June night could talk, it would probably boast it invented romance.

— Bern Williams

In June, as many as a dozen species may burst their buds on a single day. No man can heed all of these anniversaries; no man can ignore all of them.

— Aldo Leopold

In summer, the song sings itself.

— William Carlos Williams

In winter I get up at night
And dress by yellow candle-light.
In summer quite the other way
I have to go to bed by day.

— Robert Louis Stevenson

It was a splendid summer morning and it seemed as if nothing could go wrong.

— John Cheever

Knowing trees, I understand the meaning of patience. Knowing grass, I can appreciate persistence.

— Hal Borland

Life is a pure flame, and we live by an invisible sun within us.

— Thomas Browne

No bought potpourri is so pleasant as that made from ones own garden, for the petals of the flowers one has gathered at home hold the sunshine and memories of summer, and of past summers only the sunny days should be remembered.

— Eleanor Sinclair-Rhode

Oh, bring again my heart's content,
Thou Spirit of the Summer-time!

— William Allingham

Oh, the summer night
Has a smile of light
And she sits on a sapphire throne.

— Barry Cornwall

People don't notice whether it's winter or summer when they're happy.

— Anton Chekhov

Rest is not idleness, and to lie sometimes on the grass on a summer day listening to the murmur of water, or watching the clouds float across the sky, is hardly a waste of time.

— John Lubbock

Someone's sitting in the shade today because someone planted a tree a long time ago.

— Warren Buffett

Summer afternoon—summer afternoon; to me those have always been the two most beautiful words in the English language.

— Henry James

Summer is delicious. Rain is refreshing, wind braces up, snow is exhilarating; there is no such thing as bad weather, only different kinds of good weather.

— John Ruskin

Summer is the time when one sheds one's tensions with one's clothes, and the right kind of day is jeweled balm for the battered spirit. A few of those days and you can become drunk with the belief that all's right with the world.

— Ada Louise Huxtable

Summer set lip to earth's bosom bare,
And left the flushed print in a poppy there.

— Francis Thompson

The dandelions and buttercups gild all the lawn: the drowsy bee stumbles among the clover tops, and summer sweetens all to me.

— James Russell Lowell

The steady buzzzzzzz of the Katydid chorus, and the bass solo of the croaking Frog—a summer night's serenade.

— ***Michael P. Garofalo***

The Summer looks out from her brazen tower,

Through the flashing bars of July.

— ***Francis Thompson***

The summer night is like a perfection of thought.

— ***Wallace Stevens***

Then followed that beautiful season... Summer....

Filled was the air with a dreamy and magical light; and the landscape

Lay as if new created in all the freshness of childhood.

— ***Henry Wadsworth Longfellow***

There shall be eternal summer in the grateful heart.

— ***Celia Thaxter***

To believe in life is to believe there will always be someone who will water the geraniums.

— ***Flavia***

To see the Summer Sky
Is Poetry, though never in a Book it lie -
True Poems flee.

— ***Emily Dickinson***

We are much more likely to experience a sense of plenty when we are relaxed.

— ***SARK***

What dreadful hot weather we have! It keeps me in a continual state of inelegance.

— ***Jane Austen***

What is one to say about June, the time of perfect young summer, the fulfilment of the promise of the earlier months, and with as yet no sign to remind one that its fresh young beauty will ever fade.

— ***Gertrude Jekyll***

What is so rare as a day in June? Then, if ever, come perfect days.

— James Russell Lowell

When I was a little kid, of course, I was brown all summer. That's because I was free as a bird- nothing to do but catch bugs all day.

— Roy Blount Jr.

Who has not dreamed a world of bliss on a bright, sunny noon like this?

— William Howitt

Yellow butterflies look like flowers flying through the warm summer air.

— Andrea Willis

93

Teacher Quotes

Being a great teacher is very challenging and rewarding work. You have in your hands the power to influence and mould a student's mind. You have within you the capacity to instill in the child a love for learning, to keep an open mind and to keep questioning. You have the ability to promote confidence, stir thinking and awaken dreams. Here is a great collection to inspire a teacher to think, reflect and once again appreciate the importance of her work on this earth.

> A hundred years from now it will not matter what my bank account was, the sort of house I lived in, or the kind of car I drove.... but the world maybe different because I was important in the life of a child.
>
> — ***Kathy Davis***

> A teacher affects eternity; he can never tell where his influence stops.
>
> — ***Henry Brooks Adams***

> A teacher is a compass that activates the magnets of curiosity, knowledge, and wisdom in the pupils.
>
> — ***Ever Garrison***

> A teacher is one who makes himself progressively unnecessary.
>
> — ***Thomas Carruthers***

Everything should be made as simple as possible, but not simpler.

— Albert Einstein

Good teaching is more a giving of right questions than a giving of right answers.

— Josef Albers

I have been maturing as a teacher. New experiences bring new sensitivities and flexibility...

— Howard Lester

I like a teacher who gives you something to take home to think about besides homework.

— Lily Tomlin as "Edith Ann"

I touch the future. I teach.

— Christa McAuliffe

In teaching you cannot see the fruit of a day's work. It is invisible and remains so, maybe for twenty years.

— Jacques Barzun

It is important that students bring a certain ragamuffin, barefoot irreverance to their studies; they are not here to worship what is known, but to question it.

— Jacob Bronowski

It is the supreme art of the teacher to awaken joy in creative expression and knowledge.

— Albert Einstein

Kind words can be short and easy to speak, but their echoes are endless.

— Mother Teresa

Man's mind stretched by a new idea never goes back to its original dimensions.

— Oliver Wendell Holmes

No one has yet fully realised the wealth of sympathy, kindness, and generosity hidden in the soul of a child. The effort of every true education should be to unlock that treasure.

— Emma Golmam

One looks back with appreciation to the brilliant teachers, but with gratitude to those who touched our human feelings. The curriculum is so much necessary raw material, but warmth is the vital element for the growing plant and for the soul of the child.

— Carl Jung

Teaching kids to count is fine, but teaching them what counts is best.

— Bob Talbert

The art of teaching is the art of assisting discovery.

— Mark Van Doren

The dream begins with a teacher who believes in you, who tugs and pushes and leads you to the next plateau, sometimes poking you with a sharp stick called "truth.

— Dan Rather

The mediocre teacher tells. The good teacher explains. The superior teacher demonstrates. The great teacher inspires.

— William Arthur Ward

The task of the excellent teacher is to stimulate "apparently ordinary" people to unusual effort. The tough problem is not in identifying winners: it is in making winners out of ordinary people.

— K. Patricia Cross

There is no education like adversity.

— Benjamin Disraeli

To know how to suggest is the great art of teaching.

— Henri Frederic Amiel

To stimulate life, leaving it then free to develop, to unfold,herein lies the first task of the teacher.

— Maria Montessori

What the teacher is, is more important than what he teaches.

— Karl Menninger

94

Teenager Quotes

Teenage-hood can be an awkward transitional period for teenagers. So encourage them with these teen quotes. Be inspired by this straight-shooting series of teen quotes.

> A baby-sitter is a teenager who gets two dollars an hour to eat five dollars' worth of your food.
>
> – ***Henny Youngman***

> A boy becomes an adult three years before his parents think he does, and about two years after he thinks he does.
>
> – ***Lewis B. Hershey***

> Adolescents are not monsters. They are just people trying to learn how to make it among the adults in the world, who are probably not so sure themselves.
>
> – ***Virginia Satir***

> Adolescence: A stage between infancy and adultery.
>
> – ***Ambrose Bierce***

> Adolescence is perhaps nature's way of preparing parents to welcome the empty nest.
>
> – ***Karen Savage and Patricia Adams***

> As a teenager you are at the last stage in your life when you will be happy to hear that the phone is for you.
>
> – ***Fran Lebowitz***

At fourteen you don't need sickness or death for tragedy.

— *Jessamyn West*

Delight in your youth.

— *Pearl Jam*

Don't laugh at a youth for his affectations; he is only trying on one face after another to find a face of his own.

— *Logan Pearsall Smith*

Every generation laughs at the old fashions, but follows religiously the new.

— *Henry David Thoreau*

Exuberance is beautiful.

— *William Blake*

Fashion is what you adopt when you don't know who you are.

— *Quentin Crisp*

Few things are more satisfying than seeing your children have teenagers of their own.

— *Doug Larson*

Figuring out who you are is the whole point of the human experience.

— *Anna Quindlen*

Helping your eldest to pick a college is one of the greatest educational experiences of life—for the parents. Next to trying to pick his bride, it's the best way to learn that your authority, if not entirely gone, is slipping fast.

— *Sally and James Reston*

Heredity is what sets the parents of a teenager wondering about each other.

— *Laurence J. Peter*

Hmmm! Teenagers. They think they know everything. You give them an inch, and they swim all over you.

— *Sebastian, "The Little Mermaid"*

How beautiful is youth! How bright it gleams with its illusions, aspirations, dreams!

— Henry Wadsworth Longfellow

How strange that the young should always think the world is against them—when in fact that is the only time it is for them.

— Mignon McLaughlin

Human life is a continuous thread which each of us spins to his own pattern, rich and complex in meaning. There are no natural knots in it. Yet knots form, nearly always in adolescence.

— Edgar Z. Friedenberg

Keep true to the dreams of thy youth.

— Johann Friedrich von Schiller

I am every emotion times ten, I conform yet I'm rebellious, always obeying but somehow still an outlaw, always talking but never heard, I am a teenager.

— Author Unknown

I don't blame you for everything, she told me. Just the stuff my friends & I can agree on.

— Brian Andreas

I have seen my kid struggle into the kitchen in the morning with outfits that need only one accessory: an empty gin bottle.

— Erma Bombeck

I love to see a young girl go out and grab the world by the lapels.

— Maya Angelou

I never expected to see the day when girls would get sunburned in the places they do now.

— Will Rogers

If everybody is thinking alike, then somebody isn't thinking.

— General George S. Patton, Jr.

If you want to recapture your youth, just cut off his allowance.

— Al Bernstein

Incredibly, inordinately, devastatingly, immortally, calamitously, hearteningly, adorably beautiful.

— Rupert Brooke

It is hard to convince a high-school student that he will encounter a lot of problems more difficult than those of algebra and geometry.

— Edgar W. Howe

It is not chic to be too chic.

— Elsie de Wolfe

It is not in the stars to hold our destiny but in ourselves.

— William Shakespeare

Little children, headache; big children, heartache.

— Italian Proverb

Maturity begins to grow when you can sense you concern for others outweighing your concern for yourself.

— John MacNoughton

Mother Nature is providential. She gives us twelve years to develop a love for our children before turning them into teenagers.

— William Galvin

My adolescence progressed normally: enough misery to keep the death wish my usual state, an occasional high to keep me from actually taking the gas-pipe.

— Faye Moskowitz

My kids' idea of a hard life is to live in a house with only one phone.

— George Foreman

Never lend your car to anyone to whom you have given birth.

— Erma Bombeck

Small children disturb your sleep, big children your life.

— *Yiddish Proverb*

Teenagers complain there's nothing to do, then stay out all night doing it.

— *Bob Phillips*

Telling a teenager the facts of life is like giving a fish a bath.

— *Arnold H. Glasow*

The best substitute for experience is being sixteen.

— *Raymond Duncan*

The best way to keep children at home is to make the home atmosphere pleasant, and let the air out of the tires.

— *Dorothy Parker*

The invention of the teenager was a mistake. Once you identify a period of life in which people get to stay out late but don't have to pay taxes—naturally, no one wants to live any other way.

— *Judith Martin*

The teenager seems to have replaced the Communist as the appropriate target for public controversy and foreboding.

— *Edgar Friedenberg*

The troubles of adolescence eventually all go away—it's just like a really long, bad cold.

— *Dawn Ruelas*

The young always have the same problem—how to rebel and conform at the same time. They have now solved this by defying their parents and copying one another.

— *Quentin Crisp*

There isn't a child who hasn't gone out into the brave new world who eventually doesn't return to the old homestead carrying a bundle of dirty clothes.

— *Art Buchwald*

Violet will be a good color for hair at just about the same time that brunette becomes a good color for flowers.

— *Fran Lebowitz*

What a cunning mixture of sentiment, pity, tenderness, irony surrounds adolescence, what knowing watchfulness! Young birds on their first flight are hardly so hovered around.

— *Georges Bernanos*

What a shame that allowances have to stop with the teens: both those that are paid to us and those that are made for us.

— *Mignon McLaughlin*

When buying a used car, punch the buttons on the radio. If all the stations are rock and roll, there's a good chance the transmission is shot.

— *Larry Lujack*

When I was a boy of fourteen, my father was so ignorant I could hardly stand to have the old man around. But when I got to be twenty-one, I was astonished at how much he had learned in seven years.

— *Mark Twain*

You don't have to suffer to be a poet. Adolescence is enough suffering for anyone.

— *John Ciardi*

Young people are in a condition like permanent intoxication, because youth is sweet and they are growing.

— *Aristotle*

Youth is, after all, just a moment, but it is the moment, the spark that you always carry in your heart.

— *Raisa Gorbachev*

Youth! youth! how buoyant are thy hopes! they turn, like marigolds, toward the sunny side.

— *Jean Ingelow*

95

Thank You Quotes

You wll find many things in your life that fill you with thankfulness. Here is a beautiful series of thankful quotes and thank you quotes that point out the many things in your life that you can feel thankful and grateful for.

A thankful heart is not only the greatest virtue, but the parent of all other virtues.

— *Cicero*

At times our own light goes out and is rekindled by a spark from another person. Each of us has cause to think with deep gratitude of those who have lighted the flame within us.

— *Albert Schweitzer*

Be thankful for what you have; you'll end up having more. If you concentrate on what you don't have, you will never, ever have enough.

— *Oprah Winfrey*

Gratitude is something of which none of us can give too much. For on the smiles, the thanks we give, our little gestures of appreciation, our neighbors build their philosophy of life.

— *A. J. Cronin*

Gratitude unlocks the fullness of life. It turns what we have into enough, and more. It turns denial into acceptance, chaos to order, confusion to clarity. It can turn a meal into a feast, a house into a home, a stranger into a friend. Gratitude makes sense of our past, brings peace for today, and creates a vision for tomorrow.

— Melody Beattie

Develop an attitude of gratitude, and give thanks for everything that happens to you, knowing that every step forward is a step toward achieving something bigger and better than your current situation.

— Brian Tracy

Every time we remember to say "thank you", we experience nothing less than heaven on earth.

— Sarah Ban Breathnach

Feeling grateful or appreciative of someone or something in your life actually attracts more of the things that you appreciate and value into your life.

— Christiane Northrup

Gratitude helps you to grow and expand; gratitude brings joy and laughter into your life and into the lives of all those around you.

— Eileen Caddy

He is a wise man who does not grieve for the things which he has not, but rejoices for those which he has.

— Epictetus

If the only prayer you ever say in your entire life is thank you, it will be enough.

— Meister Eckhardt

If you concentrate on finding whatever is good in every situation, you will discover that your life will suddenly be filled with gratitude, a feeling that nurtures the soul.

— Rabbi Harold Kushner

In everyone's life, at some time, our inner fire goes out. It is then burst into flame by an encounter with another human being. We should all be thankful for those people who rekindle the inner spirit.

— Albert Schweitzer

In ordinary life we hardly realise that we receive a great deal more than we give, and that it is only with gratitude that life becomes rich.

— ***Dietrich Bonhoeffer***

It is impossible to feel grateful and depressed in the same moment.

— ***Naomi Williams***

Just a "thank you" is a mighty powerful prayer. Says it all.

— ***Rosie Cash***

Let us be grateful to people who make us happy; they are the charming gardeners who make our souls blossom.

— ***Marcel Proust***

Let us rise up and be thankful, for if we didn't learn a lot today, at least we learned a little, and if we didn't learn a little, at least we didn't get sick, and if we got sick, at least we didn't die; so, let us all be thankful.

— ***Buddha***

Make it a habit to tell people thank you. To express your appreciation, sincerely and without the expectation of anything in return. Truly appreciate those around you, and you'll soon find many others around you. Truly appreciate life, and you'll find that you have more of it.

— ***Ralph Marston***

No one who achieves success does so without the help of others. The wise and confident acknowledge this help with gratitude.

— ***Alfred North Whitehead***

None is more impoverished than the one who has no gratitude. Gratitude is a currency that we can mint for ourselves, and spend without fear of bankruptcy.

— ***Fred De Witt Van Amburgh***

People who live the most fulfilling lives are the ones who are always rejoicing at what they have.

— ***Richard Carlson***

So often we dwell on the things that seem impossible rather than on the things that are possible. So often we are depressed by what remains to be done and forget to be thankful for all that has been done.

— *Marian Wright Edelman*

The grateful mind is constantly fixed upon the best. Therefore it tends to become the best. It takes the form or character of the best, and will receive the best.

— *Wallace D. Wattles*

The thankful receiver bears a plentiful harvest.

— *William Blake*

The unthankful heart discovers no mercies; but the thankful heart will find, in every hour, some heavenly blessings.

— *Henry Ward Beecher*

There is a calmness to a life lived in Gratitude, a quiet joy.

— *Ralph H. Blum*

There is always, always, always something to be thankful for.

— *Author Unknown*

Things turn out best for people who make the best of the way things turn out.

— *John Wooden*

To educate yourself for the feeling of gratitude means to take nothing for granted, but to always seek out and value the kind that will stand behind the action. Nothing that is done for you is a matter of course. Everything originates in a will for the good, which is directed at you. Train yourself never to put off the word or action for the expression of gratitude.

— *Albert Schweitzer*

To live a life of gratitude is to open our eyes to the countless ways in which we are supported by the world around us.Such a life provides less space for our suffering because our attention is more balanced. We are more often occupiedwith noticing what we are given, thanking those who have helped us, and repaying the world in some concrete wayfor what we are receiving.

— *Gregg Krech*

What if you gave someone a gift, and they neglected to thank you for it—would you be likely to give them another? Life is the same way. In order to attract more of the blessings that life has to offer, you must truly appreciate what you already have.

— *Ralph Marston*

When I started counting my blessings, my whole life turned around.

— *Willie Nelson*

You simply will not be the same person two months from now after consciously giving thanks each day for the abundance that exists in your life. And you will have set in motion an ancient spiritual law: the more you have and are grateful for, the more will be given you.

— *Sarah Ban Breathnach*

You won't be happy with more until you're happy with what you've got.

— *Viki King*

96

Thought Quotes

Whether we consciously choose our thoughts or let aimlessness run our lives, sooner or later, the seeds of thoughts we have planted in our mind will bring forth. Fortunately, there's a time-delay before the thoughts that we let our lives be dominated by become realities. If not, just imagine that you consistently fear about crocodiles, and the next instant a crocodile appeared in your life! So you're given a time-delay, a pause, a second chance to choose your thoughts again. Some of these quotes are from great teachers who wrote them down ages ago. These are classic truths that will never become outdated.

A man is but the product of his thoughts. What he thinks, he becomes.

— ***Mahatma Gandhi***

A man sooner or later discovers that he is the master-gardener of his soul, the director of his life.

— ***James Allen***

All that we are is the result of what we have thought. The mind is everything. What we think, we become.

— ***Buddha***

All that you accomplish or fail to accomplish with your life is the direct result of your thoughts.

— ***James Allen***

All truly wise thoughts have been thoughts already thousands of times; but to make them truly ours, we must think them over again honestly, till they take root in our personal experience.

— Johann Wolfgang Von Goethe

Anger will never disappear so long as thoughts of resentment are cherished in the mind. Anger will disappear just as soon as thoughts of resentment are forgotten.

— Buddha

Build this day on a foundation of pleasant thoughts. Never fret at any imperfections that you fear may impede your progress. Remind yourself, as often as necessary, that you are a creature of God and have the power to achieve any dream by lifting up your thoughts. You can fly when you decide that you can. Never consider yourself defeated again. Let the vision in your heart be in your life's blueprint. Smile!

— Og Mandino

Change your thoughts, and you change your world.

— Norman Vincent Peale

Good thoughts bear good fruit, bad thoughts bear bad fruit.

— James Allen

Great thoughts reduced to practice become great acts.

— William Hazlitt

I think and that is all that I am.

— Wayne Dyer

I was a freethinker before I knew how to think.

— George Bernard Shaw

If constructive thoughts are planted positive outcomes will be the result. Plant the seeds of failure and failure will follow.

— Sidney Madwed

If you realised how powerful your thoughts are, you would never think a negative thought.

— Peace Pilgrim

Keep your feet on the ground and your thoughts at lofty heights.

— Peace Pilgrim

Let the wise guard their thoughts, which are difficult to perceive, extremely subtle, and wander at will. Thought which is well guarded is the bearer of happiness.

— Buddha

Life consists in what a person is thinking of all day.

— Ralph Waldo Emerson

Little-minded people's thoughts move in such small circles that five minutes conversation gives you an arc long enough to determine their whole curve.

— Oliver Wendell Holmes

Man is made or unmade by himself. By the right choice he ascends. As a being of power, intelligence, and love, and the lord of his own thoughts, he holds the key to every situation.

— James Allen

Most people are other people. Their thoughts are someone else's opinions, their lives a mimicry, their passions a quotation.

— Oscar Wilde

Nothing has any power over me other than that which I give it through my conscious thoughts.

— Anthony Robbins

Nurture your mind with great thoughts, for you will never go any higher than you think.

— Benjamin Disraeli

Our life is what our thoughts make it. A man will find that as he alters his thoughts toward things and other people, things and other people will alter towards him.

— James Allen

Our minds become magnetised with the dominating thoughts we hold in our minds and these magnets attract to us the forces, the people, the circumstances of life which harmonise with the nature of our dominating thoughts.

— Napoleon Hill

Our thoughts create our reality — where we put our focus is the direction we tend to go.

— Peter McWilliams

Self-disciplined begins with the mastery of your thoughts. If you don't control what you think, you can't control what you do. Simply, self-discipline enables you to think first and act afterward.

— Napoleon Hill

Some thoughts always find us young, and keep us so. Such a thought is the love of the universal and eternal beauty.

— Ralph Waldo Emerson

The game of life is the game of boomerangs. Our thoughts, deeds and words return to us sooner or later, with astounding accuracy.

— Florence Shinn

The human mind, once stretched by a new idea, never regains its original dimensions.

— Oliver Wendell Holmes

The more clear and definite you make your picture then, and the more you dwell upon it, bringing out all its delightful details, the stronger your desire will be, and the stronger your desire, the easier it will be to hold your mind fixed upon the picture of what you want.

— Wallace D. Wattles

There is a basic law that like attracts like. Negative thinking definitely attracts negative results. Conversely, if a person habitually thinks optimistically and hopefully his positive thinking sets in motion creative forces—and success instead of eluding him flows toward him.

— Norman Vincent Peale

Think twice before you speak, because your words and influence will plant the seed of either success or failure in the mind of another.

— Napoleon Hill

Thought is the sculptor who can create the person you want to be.

— Henry David Thoreau

To find yourself, think for yourself.

— Socrates

To put away aimlessness and weakness, and to begin to think with purpose, is to enter the ranks of those strong ones who only recognise failure as one of the pathways to attainment; who make all conditions serve them, and who think strongly, attempt fearlessly, and accomplish masterfully.

— James Allen

We are formed and molded by our thoughts. Those whose minds are shaped by selfless thoughts give joy when they speak or act. Joy follows them like a shadow that never leaves them.

— Buddha

We are what we think. All that we are arises With our thoughts. With our thoughts, We make our world.

— Buddha

What is the hardest thing in the world? To think.

— Ralph Waldo Emerson

What we are today comes from our thoughts of yesterday, and our present thoughts build our life of tomorrow: Our life is the creation of our mind.

— Buddha

What your heart thinks is great, is great. The soul's emphasis is always right.

— Ralph Waldo Emerson

Watch your thoughts, for they become words.

Watch your words, for they become actions.

Watch your actions, for they become habits.

Watch your habits, for they become character.

Watch your character, for it becomes your destiny.

— ***Author Unknown***

When you are inspired by some great purpose, some extraordinary project, all your thoughts break their bonds: Your mind transcends limitations, your consciousness expands in every direction, and you find yourself in a new, great, and wonderful world. Dormant forces, faculties and talents become alive, and your discover yourself to be a greater person by far than you ever dreamed yourself to be.

— ***Patanjali***

You are today where your thoughts have brought you; you will be tomorrow where your thoughts take you.

— ***James Allen***

97

Valentine Quotes

If you are single, then Valentine's Day may not be greatest time of the year for you. Seeing other people celebrating their love can make one a tad envious. However, don't be let down. Lift your sagging spirits by reading these valentine's quotes and by dreaming of your own happily-ever-after. Here is a collection of sweet love quotes to let you express your sweet adoration.

> Anyone can be passionate, but it takes real lovers to be silly.
>
> — *Rose Franken*

> For twas not into my ear you whispered
> But into my heart
> Twas not my lips you kissed
> But my soul
>
> — *Judy Garland*

> Love fails, only when we fail to love.
>
> — *J. Franklin*

> Love is an irresistible desire to be irresistibly desired.
>
> — *Robert Frost*

> Love is friendship set on fire.
>
> — *Jeremy Irons*

> Love is the enchanted dawn of every heart.
>
> — *Lamartine*

Love is the greatest refreshment in life.

— ***Pablo Picaso***

Love is the master key that opens the gates of happiness.

— ***Oliver Wendell Holmes***

Love makes your soul crawl out from its hiding place.

— ***Zora Neale Hurston***

Love unlocks doors and opens windows that weren't even there before.

— ***Mignon McLaughlin***

Love will find a way through paths where wolves fear to prey.

— ***Lord Byron***

The greatest science in the world; in heaven and on earth; is love.

— ***Mother Teresa***

The hours I spend with you I look upon as sort of a perfumed garden, a dim twilight, and a fountain singing to it. You and you alone make me feel that I am alive. Other men it is said have seen angels, but I have seen thee and thou art enough.

— ***George Moore***

There is more hunger for love and appreciation in this world than for bread.

— ***Mother Teresa***

What the world really needs is more love and less paper work.

— ***Pearl Bailey***

Where there is great love there are always miracles.

— ***Willa Cather***

No cord or cable can so forcibly draw, or hold so fast, as love can do with a twined thread.

Robert Burton

The ultimate test of a relationship is to disagree but to hold hands.

Alexandra Penney

No one can understand love who has not experienced infatuation. And no one can understand infatuation, no matter how many times he has experienced it.

Mignon McLaughlin

The lover is a monotheist who knows that other people worship different gods but cannot himself imagine that there could be other gods.

Theodor Reik

A kiss is the shortest distance between two.

Henny Youngman

I have found men who didn't know how to kiss. I've always found time to teach them.

Mae West

It is the same in love as in war; a fortress that parleys is half taken.

Marguerite de Valois

It is the things in common that make relationships enjoyable, but it is the little differences that make them interesting.

Todd Ruthman

Love looks not with the eyes, but with the mind,

And therefore is winged Cupid painted blind.

William Shakespeare

Falling in love is so hard on the knees.

Aerosmith

In the arithmetic of love, one plus one equals everything, and two minus one equals nothing.

Mignon McLaughlin

The heart has reasons that reason does not understand.

Jacques Benigne Bossuel

And when the future hinges on the next words that are said, don't let logic interfere, believe your heart instead.

Philip Robinson

We are, each of us angels with only one wing; and we can only fly by embracing one another.

Luciano de Crescenzo

Love is not blind—it sees more, not less. But because it sees more, it is willing to see less.

Julins Gordon

Love is composed of a single soul inhabiting two bodies.

Aristotle

98

Vacation Quotes

To many of us, some of the favorite memories consist of past family vacations. The funny incidents, the little mishaps, the closeness shared, all these weaved a good story for the heart. Here is a collection of wonderful vacation quotes to put you into a holiday mood and also to remind you of what's important when you go on a trip.

A good vacation is over when you begin to yearn for your work.

— ***Morris Fishbein***

A travel adventure has no substitute. It is the ultimate experience, your one big opportunity for flair.

— ***Rosalind Massow***

A traveller am I and a navigator, and every day I discover a new region within my soul.

— ***Kahlil Gibran***

A traveller without observation is a bird without wings.

— ***Moslih Eddin Saadi***

A trip is what you take when you can't take anymore of what you've been taking.

— ***Adeline Ainsworth***

A vacation frequently means that the family goes away for a rest, accompanied by mother, who sees that the others get it.

— ***Marcelene Cox***

A vacation is like love—anticipated with pleasure, experienced with discomfort, and remembered with nostalgia.

— ***Author Unknown***

A vacation is a sunburn at premium prices.

— ***Hal Chadwicke***

A vacation is what you take when you can no longer take what you've been taking.

— ***Earl Wilson***

Adventures are to the adventurous.

— ***Benjamin Disraeli***

Babies don't need a vacation but I still see them at the beach. I'll go over to them and say, 'What are you doing here, you've never worked a day in your life!'.

— ***Stephen Wright***

Be an explorer. The universe is filled with wonder and magical things.

— ***Flavia***

Better to ask twice than lose your way once.

— ***Danish Proverb***

Find what brings you joy and go there.

— ***Jan Phillips***

For travel to be delightful, one must have a good place to leave and return to.

— ***Frederick B. Wilcox***

He who returns from a journey is not the same as he who left.

— ***Chinese Proverb***

I am one of those who never knows the direction of my journeyuntil I have almost arrived.

— ***Anna Louise Strong***

I can't think of anything that excites a great sense of childlike wonder than to be in a country where you are ignorant of almost everything.

— ***Bill Bryson***

I hoped that the trip would be the best of all journeys: a journey into ourselves.

— ***Shirley MacLaine***

If you reject the food, ignore the customs, fear the religion and avoid the people, you might better stay home.

— ***James Michener***

Isn't it interesting that people feel best about themselves right before they go on vacation? They've cleared up all of their to-do piles, closed up transactions, renewed old promises with themselves. My most basic suggestion is that people should do that more than just once a year.

— ***David Allen***

It began in mystery, and it will end in mystery, but what a savage and beautiful country lies in between.

— ***Diane Ackerman***

It is good to have an end to journey toward, but it is the journey that matters in the end.

— ***Ursula K. LeGuin***

No man needs a vacation so much as the person who has just had one.

— ***Elbert Hubbard***

No matter what happens, travel gives you a story to tell.

— ***Jewish Proverb***

Once you have travelled, the voyage never ends, but is played out over and over again in the quietest chambers... the mind can never break off from the journey.

— ***Author Unknown***

There is no surer way to find out whether you like people or hate them than to travel with them.

— ***Mark Twain***

There is nothing like returning to a place that remains unchanged to find the ways in which you yourself have altered.

— ***Nelson Mandela***

Those that say you can't take it with you never saw a car packed for a vacation trip.

– Author Unknown

Though we travel the world over to find the beautiful, we must carry it with us or we find it not.

– Ralph Waldo Emerson

Travel makes one modest, you see what a tiny place you occupy in the world.

– Gustave Flaubert

Travelling is almost like talking with men of other centuries.

– Rene' Descartes

Travelling is not just seeing the new; it is also leaving behind. Not just opening doors; also closing them behind you, never to return. But the place you have left forever is always there for you to see whenever you shut your eyes.

– Jan Myrdal

You can fall in love at first sight with a place as well as a person.

– Alec Waugh

99

Wedding Quotes

Getting married is probably one of the most important decisions a woman can ever make in her life. It certainly takes courage to finally decide your man is the right one for you and to share the rest of your life with him. Here is a meaningful and sometimes humorous collection of quotes about wedding. If you are looking for wedding quotes for your about-to-wed or newly-wed friends, cards, scrapbooks, letters or well-wishes, these wedding quotes will work beautifully too.

> A good marriage is that in which each appoints the other guardian of his solitude.
>
> — ***Rainer Maria Rilke***

> A successful marriage requires falling in love many times, always with the same person.
>
> — ***Germaine Greer***

> Are we not like two volumes of one book?
>
> — ***Marceline Desbordes-Valmore***

> Grow old with me! The best is yet to be.
>
> — ***Robert Browning***

> Happy and thrice happy are those who enjoy an uninterrupted union, and whose love, unbroken by any sour complaints, shall not dissolve until the last day of their existence.
>
> — ***Horace***

I dreamed of a wedding of elaborate elegance,
A church filled with family and friends.
I asked him what kind of a wedding he wished for,
He said one that would make me his wife.

— Author Unknown

I love being married. It's so great to find that one special person you want to annoy for the rest of your life.

— Rita Rudner

In all of the wedding cake, hope is the sweetest of plums.

— Douglas Jerrold

In marriage, everyday you love, and everyday you forgive. It is an ongoing sacrament, love and forgiveness.

— Bill Moyers

It took great courage to ask a beautiful young woman to marry me. Believe me, it is easier to play the whole Petrushka on the piano.

— Arthur Rubinstein

Let us celebrate the occasion with wine and sweet words.

— Plautus

Marriage—a book of which the first chapter is written in poetry and the remaining chapters written in prose.

— Beverly Nichols

Marriage is an Athenic weaving together of families, of two souls with their individual fates and destinies, of time and eternity—everyday life married to the timeless mysteries of the soul.

— Thomas Moore

Marrying a man is like buying something you've been admiring for a long time in a shop window. You may love it when you get home, but it doesn't always go with everything else in the house.

— Jean Kerr

My Greatest wish for the two of you is that through the years your love for each other will so deepen and grow, that years from now you will look back on this day, your wedding day, as the day you loved each other the least.

— Wedding Toast, to the Bride and Groom

Now join hands, and with your hands your hearts.

— William Shakespeare

Success in marriage does not come merely through finding the right mate, but through being the right mate.

— Barnett Brickner

The sum which two married people owe to one another defies calculation. It is an infinite debt, which can only be discharged through all eternity.

— Johann Wolfgang von Goethe

There is no more lovely, friendly and charming relationship, communion or company than a good marriage.

— Martin Luther

There is nothing nobler or more admirable than when two people who see eye to eye keep house as man and wife, confounding their enemies and delighting their friends.

— Homer

This day I will marry my friend, the one I laugh with, live for, dream with, love.

— Anonymous

To have and to hold from this day forward, for better or worse, for richer for poorer, in sickness and in health, to love and to cherish to death do us part.

— Book of Common Prayer

To keep your marriage brimming, with love in the wedding cup, whenever you're wrong, admit it; whenever you're right, shut up.

— Ogden Nash

Two souls with but a single thought,
Two hearts that beat as one.

— ***Friedrich Halm***

Two such as you with such a master speed cannot be parted nor be swept away from one another once you are agreed that life is only life forevermore together wing to wing and oar to oar.

— ***Robert Frost***

We've got this gift of love, but love is like a precious plant. You can't just accept it and leave it in the cupboard or just think it's going to get on by itself. You've got to keep watering it. You've got to really look after it and nurture it.

— ***John Lennon***

Whatever souls are made of, his and mine are the same.

— ***Emily Bronte***

When you make a sacrifice in marriage, you're sacrificing not to each other but to unity in a relationship.

— ***Joseph Campbell***

When you meet someone who can cook and do housework—don't hesitate a minute—marry him.

— ***Author Unknown***

[W]hen you realise you want to spend the rest of your life with somebody, you want the rest of your life to start as soon as possible.

— ***Nora Ephron, When Harry Met Sally***

With this ring I thee wed, with my body I thee worship, and with all my worldly goods I thee endow.

— ***Book of Common Prayer***

100

Wife Quotes

Being a wife can be a challenge and one of the biggest roles that a woman can take on. It is easier to be loving during the early years of a relationship where everything is fresh and new. It takes commitment and dedication to remain loving in a long marriage, especially one where the busyness of daily life and children can be overwhelming at times. This collection will make you smile, make you feel good and take pride in being a wife.

A faithful and loving wife is the jewel of a marriage.

— *Lamar Cole*

A man's wife has more power over him than the state has.

— *Ralph Waldo Emerson*

A wife is essential to great longevity; she is the receptacle of half a man's cares, and two-thirds of his ill-humour.

— *Charles Reade*

A wife is the joy of a man's heart.

— *Talmud*

Let the wife make the husband glad to come home, and let him make her sorry to see him leave.

— *Martin Luther King*

Let us now set forth one of the fundamental truths about marriage: the wife is in charge.

— *Bill Cosby*

My best chosen friend, companion, guide, to walk through life, linked hand-in-hand, two equal, loving friends, true husband and true wife.

— Sir Charles Gavan Duffy

My most brilliant achievement was my ability to be able to persuade my wife to marry me.

— Winston Churchill

My wife runs the house much better than I could so I think she could be a linesman or a referee or even a football manager and that's the truth.

— Ian Holloway

No man succeeds without a good woman behind him. Wife or mother, if it is both, he is twice blessed indeed.

— Harold Macmillan

Of all the home remedies, a good wife is best.

— Kin Hubbard

One should choose a wife with the ears, rather than with the eyes.

— French Proverb

Only two things are necessary to keep one's wife happy. One is to let her think she is having her own way, and the other is to let her have it.

— Lyndon Johnson

The man who says his wife can't take a joke, forgets that she took him...

— Oscar Wilde

When a man says it's a silly childish game, it's probably something his wife can beat him at.

Don Epperson

Wives are young men's mistresses, companions for middle age, and old men's nurses.

— Francis Bacon

101

Work Quotes

In order to be really good and successful at something, we have to enjoy doing it. If you don't, oftentimes you will find yourself not being very successful at it. Work gives people a sense of purpose. It is not uncommon for work to be a large part of a person's life. People need to feel accomplished, successful and work allows us to strive for our best and to enjoy the fruits of our labor. This collection of work quotes will jar your thoughts and make you think about the importance of loving what you do.

Being busy does not always mean real work. The object of all work is production or accomplishment and to either of these ends there must be forethought, system, planning, intelligence, and honest purpose, as well as perspiration. Seeming to do is not doing.

– Thomas Alva Edison

Concentrate all your thoughts upon the work at hand. The sun's rays do not burn until brought to a focus.

– Alexander Graham Bell

Derive happiness in oneself from a good day's work, from illuminating the fog that surrounds us.

– Henri Matisse

Dictionary is the only place that success comes before work. Hard work is the price we must pay for success.

I think you can accomplish anything if you're willing to pay the price.

— Vince Lombardi

Do what you love. When you love your work, you become the best worker in the world.

— Uri Geller

Doing what you love is the cornerstone of having abundance in your life.

— Dr. Wayne Dyer

Don't waste life in doubts and fears; spend yourself on the work before you, well assured that the right performance of this hour's duties will be the best preparation for the hours and ages that will follow it.

— Ralph Waldo Emerson

Everyone has been made for some particular work, and the desire for that work has been put in every heart.

— Jalal ad-Din Rumi

Far and away the best prize that life offers is the chance to work hard at work worth doing.

— Theodore Roosevelt

Find something you love to do and you'll never have to work a day in your life.

— Harvey MacKay

Genius is one percent inspiration and ninety-nine percent perspiration.

— Thomas Alva Edison

I don't wait for moods. You accomplish nothing if you do that. Your mind must know it has got to get down to work.

— Pearl S. Buck

I enjoy my work so much that I have to be pulled away from my work into leisure.

— Ralph Nader

I feel sorry for the person who can't get genuinely excited about his work. Not only will he never be satisfied, but he will never achieve anything worthwhile.

— ***Walter Chrysler***

I like to build things, I like to do things. I am having a lot of fun.

— ***Walter Chrysler***

If A equals success, then the formula is A equals X plus Y and Z, with X being work, Y play, and Z keeping your mouth shut.

— ***Albert Einstein***

I'm a great believer in luck and I find the harder I work, the more I have of it.

— ***Thomas Jefferson***

In order that people may be happy in their work, these three things are needed: they must be fit for it; they must not do too much of it; and they must have a sense of success in it.

— ***John Ruskin***

It's not the hours you put in your work that counts, it's the work you put in the hours.

— ***Sam Ewing***

Never continue in a job you don't enjoy. If you're happy in what you're doing, you'll like yourself, you'll have inner peace. And if you have that, along with physical health, you will have had more success than you could possibly have imagined.

— ***Johnny Carson***

Never work just for money or for power. They won't save your soul or help you sleep at night.

— ***Marian Wright Edelman***

Nobody can be successful unless he loves his work.

— ***David Sarnoff***

One must work and dare if one really wants to live.

— ***Vincent van Gogh***

Pleasure in the job puts perfection in the work.

— Aristotle

Real success is finding your lifework in the work that you love.

— David McCullough

Surround yourself with people who take their work seriously, but not themselves, those who work hard and play hard.

— Colin Powell

Talent is cheaper than table salt. What separates the talented individual from the successful one is a lot of hard work.

— Stephen King

The big secret in life is that there is no big secret. Whatever your goal, you can get there if you're willing to work.

— Oprah Winfrey

The biggest mistake people make in life is not trying to make a living at doing what they most enjoy.

— Malcolm Forbes

The man who does not work for the love of work but only for money is not likely to make money nor find much fun in life.

— Charles Schwab

The secret of joy in work is contained in one word— excellence. To know how to do something well is to enjoy it.

— Pearl S. Buck

The true way to render ourselves happy is to love our work and find in it our pleasure.

— Francoise de Motteville

There is joy in work. There is no happiness except in the realisation that we have accomplished something.

— Henry Ford

Think not of yourself as the architect of your career but as the sculptor. Expect to have to do a lot of hard hammering and chiseling and scraping and polishing.

— BC Forbes

This was work (music industry) but it was the awakening to what was to become a life's passion.

— Clive Davis

Three Rules of Work:

Out of clutter find simplicity;

From discord find harmony;

In the middle of difficulty lies opportunity.

— Albert Einstein

We work to become, not to acquire.

— Elbert Hubbard

What is it that you like doing? If you don't like it, get out of it, because you'll be lousy at it. You don't have to stay with a job for the rest of your life, because if you don't like it you'll never be successful in it.

— Lee Iacocca

When love and skill work together, expect a masterpiece.

— John Ruskin

When your work speaks for itself, don't interrupt.

— Henry J. Kaiser

Whenever it is in any way possible, every boy and girl should choose as his life work some occupation which he should like to do anyhow, even if he did not need the money.

— William Lyon Phelps

Without work, all life goes rotten. But when work is soulless, life stifles and dies.

— Albert Camus

Work joyfully and peacefully, knowing that right thoughts and right efforts will inevitably bring about right results.

— James Allen

Work is either fun or drudgery. It depends on your attitude. I like fun.

— Colleen C. Barrett

Work is love made visible. And if you cannot work with love but only with distaste, it is better that you should leave your work and sit at the gate of the temple and take alms of those who work with joy.

— Kahlil Gibran

Work while it is called today, for you know not how much you will be hindered tomorrow. One today is worth two tomorrow's; never leave that till tomorrow which you can do today.

— Benjamin Franklin

Work while you have the light. You are responsible for the talent that has been entrusted to you.

— Henri Frederic Amiel

You have to put in many, many, many tiny efforts that nobody sees or appreciates before you achieve anything worthwhile.

— Brian Tracy

Your work is to discover your world and then with all your heart give yourself to it.

— Buddha

You've got to love what you do to really make things happen.

— Philip Green

102

Women Quotes

If you like reading philosophical quotes, here are some great philosophical women quotes. Famous women leaders like Mother Teresa, Emily Dickinson, Golda Meir, Aung San Suu Kyi, among others have expressed their philosophical views. Their breadth of awareness and depth of wisdom is sure to leave you impressed.

We are all pencils in the hand of God writing love letters to the world.

Mother Theresa

It's not catastrophes, murders, deaths, diseases, that age and kill us; it's the way people look and laugh, and run up the steps of omnibuses.

Virginia Woolf

Sometimes questions are more important than answers.

Nancy Willard

The soul should always stand ajar, ready to welcome the ecstatic experience.

Emily Dickinson

The problem that has no name — which is simply the fact that American women are kept from growing to their full human capacities — is taking a far greater toll on the physical and mental health of our country than any known disease.

Betty Friedan

She had been forced into prudence in her youth, she learned romance as she grew older—the natural sequence of an unnatural beginning.

Jane Austen

You are unique, and if that is not fulfilled then something has been lost.

Martha Graham

The greater your capacity to love, the greater is your capacity to feel the pain.

Jennifer Aniston

When will our consciences grow so tender that we will act to prevent human misery rather than avenge it?

Eleanor Roosevelt

Those who don't know how to weep with their whole heart don't know how to laugh either.

Golda Meir

Deliver me from your cold phlegmatic preachers, politicians, friends, lovers and husbands.

Abigail Adams

Old age is no place for sissies.

Bette Davis

I make the most of all that comes and the least of all that goes.

Sara Teasdale

Love often leads to healing, while fear and isolation breed illness. And our biggest fear is abandonment.

Cunduce Perl

One's prime is elusive. You little girls, when you grow up, must be on the alert to recognise your prime at whatever time of your life it may occur.

Muriel Spark

The education and empowerment of women throughout the world cannot fail to result in a more caring, tolerant, just and peaceful life for all.

Aung San Suu Kyi

A bird doesn't sing because it has an answer, it sings because it has a song.

Maya Angelou

The future belongs to those who believe in the beauty of their dreams.

Eleanor Roosevelt

Lasting change is a series of compromises. And compromise is all right, as long your values don't change.

Jane Goodall

Freedom is always and exclusively freedom for the one who thinks differently.

Rosa Luxemburg

We think sometimes that poverty is only being hungry, naked and homeless. The poverty of being unwanted, unloved and uncared for is the greatest poverty. We must start in our own homes to remedy this kind of poverty.

Mother Teresa

Pure love is a willingness to give without a thought of receiving anything in return.

Peace Pilgrim

I've given my memoirs far more thought than any of my marriages. You can't divorce a book.

Gloria Swanson

Other Books on

WORD POWER SERIES

1. Idiomatic English (How to Write & Speak It) **(New)**	175/-
2. School Essays, Letters, Applications, Paragraphs, and Stories For Higher Secondary Students **(New)**	110/-
3. Effective English Comprehention Read Fast, Understand Better! **(New)**	160/-
4. Latest Essays for College & Competitive Examinations **(New)**	150/-
5. Dictionary of New Words **(New)**	125/-
6. Art of English Conversation Speak English Fluently **(New)**	125/-
7. Teach Yourself English Grammar & Composition **(New)**	125/-
8. Common & Uncommon Proverbs **(New)**	125/-
9. Effective Editing Help Yourself in Becoming a Good Editor **(New)**	150/-
10. Effective English A Boon for Learners **(New)**	125/-
11. Essays for Primary Classes	60/-
12. Essays for Junior Classes	60/-
13. Essays for Senior Classes	60/-
14. Dictionary of Synonyms and Antonyms	150/-
15. Dictionary of Idioms and Phrases	150/-
16. Common Phrases	125/-
17. How to Write & Speak Correct English	150/-
18. Meaningful Quotes	175/-
19. Punctuation Book	125/-
20. Top School Essays	110/-
21. How to Write Business Letters with CD	250/-
22. Everyday Grammar	150/-
23. Everyday Conversation	150/-
24. Letters for All Occasions	125/-
25. School Essays & Letters for Juniors	110/-
26. Common Mistakes in English	125/-
27. The Power of Writing	150/-
28. Learn English in 21 Lessons	125/-
29. First English Dictionary	125/-
30. Boost Your Spelling Power	125/-

31. Self-Help to English Conversation	150/-
32. The Art of Effective Communication	125/-
33. A Book of Proverbs & Quotations	110/-
34. Word Power Made Easy	160/-
35. English Grammar Easier Way	160/-
36. General English for Competitive Examinations	160/-
37. Spoken English	125/-
38. School Essays, Letters Writing and Phrases	125/-
39. How to Write & Speak Better English	125/-
40. Quote Unquote (A Handbook of Famous Quotations)	160/-
41. Improve Your Vocabulary	150/-
42. Common Errors in English	150/-
43. The Art of Effective Letter Writing	125/-
44. Synonyms & Antonyms	125/-
45. Idioms	125/-
46. Business Letters	125/-

Unit No. 220, 2nd Floor, 4735/22, Prakash Deep Building,
Ansari Road, Darya Ganj, New Delhi- 110002
Ph.: 32903912, 23280047, 9811594448
E-mail : lotuspress1984@gmail.com, www.lotuspress.co.in